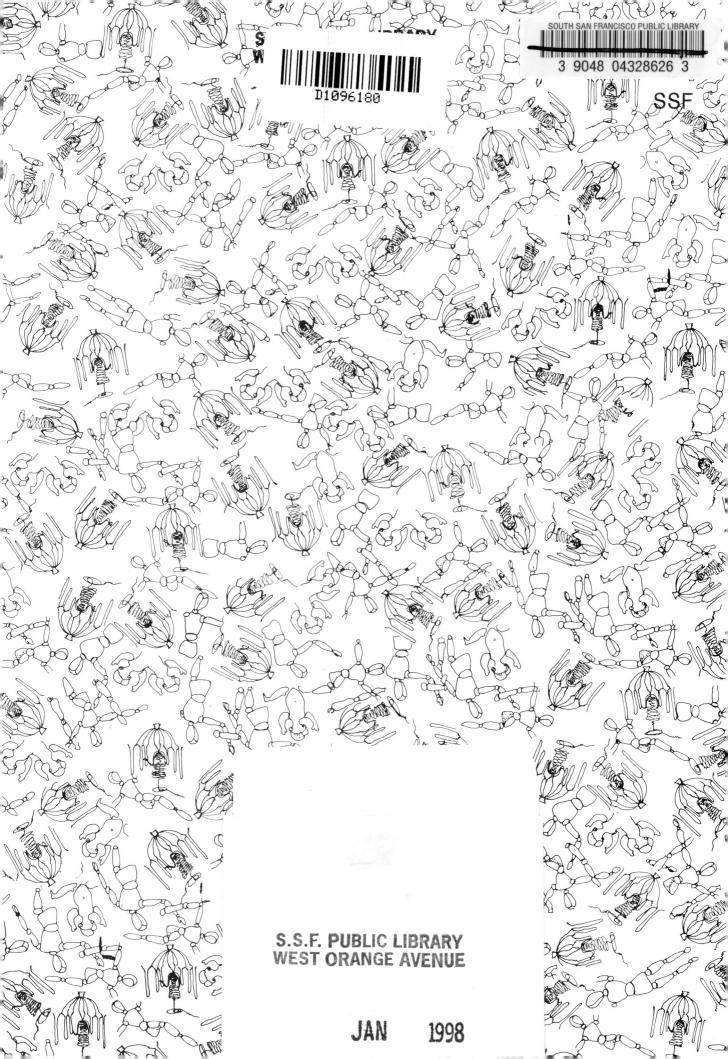

THE TWENTIETH CENTURY HISTORIES OF FASHION

Series edited by
Ieri Attualità

THE TWENTIETH CENTURY
FASHION AND DRESS
Tentative titles

WOMAN

1. Evening dresses 1900 ... 1940 (Marco Tosa)
2. Evening dresses 1940 ... (Marco Tosa)
3. Maternity fashion (Doretta Davanzo Poli)
4. Skirts & more skirts (Flora Gandolfi)
5. Costume jewellery
6. Shoes for special occasions
7. Details: sleeves
8. Strictly personal: corsets and brassières
9. Petticoats & co.
10. Nightwear
11. Trousers for women
12. Day and evening bags
13. Blouses
14. Large and small hats
15. Hosiery and related items
16. Gloves
17. Cloaks and coats
18. Light coats and raincoats
19. Accessories for ladies: umbrellas and canes
20. Hairstyles
21. You can do anything with fur vol. 1
22. You can do anything with fur vol. 2
23. Casual shoes and boots
24. Afternoon and cocktail dresses
25. Shawls, scarfs and silk squares
26. Bridal gowns
27. Work-clothes
28. Beachwear and swimsuits
29. Details: necks and necklines
30. Belts and artificial flowers
31. Suits and daywear
32. Tricot and jersey fashions

CHILDREN

33. Children in their party dress (Nora Villa)
34. Girls
35. Children and brats
36. Children's shoes
37. Teenage boys
38. Teenage girls
39. Babies

MEN

40. Men's hats (Giuliano Folledore)
41. Furs for Men (Anna Municchi)
42. Trousers & co. (Vittoria de Buzzaccarini)
43. Work-clothes
44. Underwear
45. Shirts
46. Men's accessories: belts, gloves, ties and scarfs
47. Jackets
48. Waistcoats
49. Men's jewellery
50. Raincoats, ponchos and k-ways
51. Umbrellas, sticks and canes
52. Overcoats and coats
53. Pyjamas, robes etc.
54. Knitwear: cardigans and pullovers
55. Sportswear
56. Hairstyles, beards and mustaches
57. Shoes and boots
58. Uniforms
59. Suitcases, briefcases and bags
60. Swimsuits
61. Casualwear: blouson jackets and cabans

SPECIAL ITEMS

62. The handkerchief
63. Buttons
64. Ribbons round the world
65. Leather clothing
66. Jeans
67. T- and polo shirt
68. Glasses

FABRICS

69. Fabrics in fashions: cotton
70. Fabrics in fashions: wool
71. Fabrics in fashions: silk
72. Fabrics in fashions: man-made fabrics

VITTORIA de BUZZACCARINI · ISABELLA ZOTTI MINICI

Buttons & sundries

ZanfiEditori

ACKNOWLEDGEMENTS

Vittoria de Buzzaccarini and Isabella Zotti Minici would like to thank the following people for their kind cooperation:

Silvia, Valerio, Riccardo and Elisabetta Bisello: Giorgio Busetto - director of the Fondazione Querini Stampalia, Venice - Grazietta Butazzi, Silvia Corinaldi of Bomisa, Sergio and Stefano Cannara, Carlo and Liana Carnevali, Doretta Davanzo Poli, Michaela de Favari, Angelo Fenili, Giuliano Fratti, Daniela Fugazza Stagni, Fiora Gandolfi and Helenio Herrera, Romano Goni of Miban, Toni Grossi, Franco Jacassi, Giovanni Lanfranchi Spa, Stefania Moronato, director of the Costume Museum, Palazzo Mocenigo, Venice - Giorgio Moschino, Anna Municchi, Chiara Padovano, Paolo Peri, Francesco Rapazzini de Buzzaccarini, Giampaolo Rizzetto, Giandomenico Romanelli - director of the Municipal Museums of Venice - Sandra and Maria Simionato, Angelo Secchi, Willy Zavaritt, and special thanks go to the publisher Celestino Zanfi, Elena Vezzalini, Giuliano Grossi and all the collaborators at Zanfi Editori, Modena.

ICONOGRAPHIC AND PHOTOGRAPHIC REFERENCES

Buttons at n. 1, 12, 17, 18, 19, 26, 28, 30, and 37 belong to Carlo and Liana Carnevali's collection, Florence.

Buttons at n. 11, 20, 30, 33, 36, 37, 38, 43, 50, 56, 57, 60, 64, 72, 75, 78, 80, 83, 86, 99, 100, 101, 102, 109, 110, 114, 121, 123, 131, 133, 160, 161, 162, 203, 205, 207, 208, 212, 226 and 227 belong to Romano Goni of Miban's collection, Parma. Photos: Ivano Medici and Giuliano Grossi.

Buttons at n. 13, 32, 41, 44, 47, 48, 62, 68, 75, 77, 78, 79, 84, 85, 87, 88, 90, 91, 95, 98, 104, 108, 109, 111, 120, 149, 151, 153, 166, 167, 206, 209, 210, 211, 226 and 227 belong to Vittoria de Buzzaccarini's collection. Photos: Ivano Medici, Giuliano Grossi and Teodoro Selianitis.

Pictures at n. 21, 31, 42, 54 and 148 are taken from the *Donazione Tirelli* catalogue. Photos: Mario Carrieri.

Buttons at n. 30, 33, 43, 58, 61, 165, 204, 225 published by *Almanac*, belong to the *Tender Buttons* collection. Photos: Mark Lyon.

All photographic reproduction is by Ivano Medici and Giuliano Grossi.

Coordination: Vittoria de Buzzaccarini
Compilation: Alessandra de Nitto, Angelo Secchi, Elena Vezzalini
Historical Research: Isabella Zotti Minici
Iconographic Research: Michaela de Favari, Chiara Padovano
Page layout: Michaela de Favari
Graphic design: Giuliano Grossi
Cover: Studio Cancelli
Translation: F.Hurdis Jones

INDEX

THE HISTORICAL BACKGROUND

1.

A FEW QUOTATIONS

The origin of buttons is lost in the mists of prehistory. Their Bronze-age prototypes were not very different from those immortalized much later, in the 20th century of our era, by Field Marshal Montgomery: the long, olive-shaped wooden buttons he wore on his camel-hair duffel coat, held in place by leather thongs passing through a central hole.

Recent archaeological finds have revealed that the German tribes were using, in 500 B.C. clothes-fastenings similar to the cuff-links we know today, formed of two plates joined by a rigid stem. The German version was often made from a small animal bone, the "heads" of which served as buttons.

The fact that these people had hit upon a device for fastening their tunics and breeches finds confirmation in the etymology of the word button, from the Germanic *botan*, whence, with variations, it has passed into so many languages.

The word first appears in writing in the 12th century *Chanson de Roland* which states that *conseils d'orgueil ne vaut nie un boton*, showing the Middle Ages thought of a button as something small and worthless.

1. Iron button, 18th century.

"A small flat or convex disc, or a small ball of varying materials, used to hold together different portions of clothing or other surfaces", according to the authoritative *Vocabolario degli Accademici della Crusca*, "and, by analogy, any round protuberance in the shape of a button, such, for instance, as the stud at the point of a fencing-foil", continues the dictionary, thus reassuring fencers. For the benefit of clerical readers, the work adds: "the fastening of cope worn by Bishops and Popes is also called a button".

"Button is also used to describe a pill composed of various medical ingredients for infusions or for boiling in spirits": here "medical ingredients" should read "aromatics", perhaps for help in digestive difficulties, toothache or other troubles that can be soothed by a glass of "sweet

3.

2. The great shower-off of buttons in the Middle Ages were the Turks and Ottomans, who passed the fashion on the Crusaders. G. Ferrario, *Il costume di tutti i popoli antichi e moderni.*

3. This Merovingian coin shows Lothair who fastens his mantle with three buttons, on the shoulders and the front. G. Ferrario *op. cit.*

spirits". The Academy's definitions becomes poetic when we read that "the buds of certain flowers, such as roses, are known as buttons", and quotes "two cheeks like the sweet-smelling buttons of a rose". And the slangy connotations of the word abound: "not to care a brass button", "to be a button short (to be not all there)"; "buttons" for a page-boy; "buttons" as the excreta of sheep or goats: the word indeed buttonholes (or better), button-holds us firmly.

But leaving aside slang and poetry, the button remains, for most people, an essential accessory for fastening their clothes, and, as such, forms part of the history of fashion.

THE REAL STORY

Knowledge of the use and manufacture of buttons found a decisive impulse in the return of the Crusaders, who imported Turkish tastes, including the copious use of buttons. Even some centuries later, Francesco Berni, in his *Rime Burlesche,* advises the reader to wear "a Turkish robe, with buttons and buttonholes down to the ground". The real story begins in the 13th century, when fashion suggested high-waisted dresses with clinging sleeves that gave women's bodies more height and grace. The sleeves were cut close to the arm, and called for tight, buttoned fastenings.

An otherwise obscure *maître* called Mace Maillard finds his place in the history of costume because of his tomb-effigy in a Breton church, showing him with a series of little buttons along the outside of his narrow sleeves.

4. Decoration of buttons and on a silver-gilt statue dated 1375. Venice. *Tesoro di S. Marco.*

5.

5. Fifteenth-century elegance called for a profusion of buttons on "giornee" and "albernie". Pisanello, *Costume studies*. Chantilly, *Musée Condé*.

6. Pearl and gold buttons, valuable fastenings for huge sleeves. V. Carpaccio, *Apotheosis of St. Ursula*, details, 1491, Venice, *Galleria dell' Accademia*.

7. Raphael's beautiful lady fastens her gay sleeves with precious gold and ruby buttons. R. Sanzio (attributed) 1518. *Portrait of Juana of Aragon*, detail. Paris, *Musée du Louvre*.

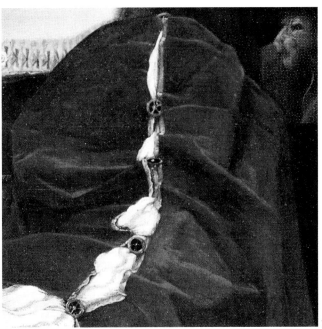

6.

7.

Oddly, buttons were only used in the Middle Ages as sleeve-fastenings, almost never on the back or front of clothes. This obliged ladies, especially, to go through complicated contortions when pulling over their heads garments that only rarely had one or two buttons at the collar.

The *Registri dei Mestieri* drawn up in the mid-13th century by Etienne Bouileau, provost of Paris, includes the guild of *boutonniers*, side by side with that of the dice-makers. From the beginning, the button-makers' corporation had statutes reflecting the requirements of the workers, as well as those of the government. A "board" of eleven members oversaw the application of these rules, whereby an "honest" young man of at least seventeen, legitimate by birth and both whose parents were known to the guild, could become an apprentice. For the honour of learning his trade, he paid a tenth of his wages to the King and a fifth to the corporation. Heavy fines fell upon him for non-payment, or from exceeding the limitations the guild imposed on him: for instance, if he belonged to the metal-buttonmakers' corporation but made buttons of ivory or other materials, and also if he worked on holidays or in the evenings after the announcement by the

town crier that "night has fallen and all's well".

Button-makers were subdivided into *paternotriers*, who were responsible for horn, bone and ivory buttons; *boutonniers* who worked in various metals like iron or *archal* (an alloy which was probably brass much used over three centuries); and *orfèvres*, who used precious metals or glass. The guild's statutes absolutely forbade the manufacture of *ersioz*, that is to say asymetrical buttons: half of each button must be equal to the other half according to the rules, and infractions led to a fine and confiscation of the irregular articles.

The same held true in Italy: Venice had a corporation of *coroneri* and *anemeri*, of which the first produced "grains" for rosaries and the second "button-cores", which were in most cases covered in the material of the clothes they were designed to adorn. So that button-making was by no means a marginal activity, but one element of that European craft-economy which lasted until after the French Revolution, when libertarian proclamations marked the end of codified craft-regulations through Europe, replacing them with a more autonomous form of labour-management.

INVESTMENT CAPITAL

In a very short time, the little accessory ceased to be that, and was replaced by precious metals and stones.

The first *pomelli* or *maspilli* were more essential than frivolous, but soon the buttons of the Middle Ages became ornamental, of valuable materials, like the silver ones that decorated men's *guarnacche*, long squared open -fronted tunics. Valuable buttons are mentioned in the inventories of rich men, and naturally in those of kings: Saint Louis IX took part in the Crusade wearing a coat given him by the Sultan, much admired for its profusion of solid gold *noiaus*.

In the 14th century, *sieur Pierre*, a French goldsmith, received an order for twenty gold buttons to fasten a lady's dress, and nine series of buttons for her husband, one of which had fifty gold *péroli* (pear-shaped buttons), as well as many pearls.

The Monza inventories of the 15th century mention four jackets with gold buttons "varying from 40 to 126 in number", returned to the widow of Nicola Lugoza, executed for conspiring against the Duke of Milan. Silver-gilt or pearl buttons ran up ladies' mantles "for the length of a shoulder towards the throat".

These buttons were called *péroli* with evident reference to the fruit; they were made of silver, gold, coral, amber and pearls. Buttonholes were ornamental too, and were often made of silver. All this gave rise to persecution by sumptuary laws, which have always tried in vain to regulate and condemn florid clothing, even in matter of details, as can be seen from the regulations of the Company of the Holy Cross in Prato, which was already laying it down in the 13th century that "no member of the Company shall wear red or yellow cloth, nor show off buttons of anything but cloth". In June 1334, a law of the Venetian Senate stated that "men above the age of ten" must not decorate their clothes with trimmings and lace, pearls, gold or silver, but only with silver *péroli*.

Naturally, wasteful expenditure on luxury objects was looked down upon: in the inventory drawn up for the dowry of Caterina Porta, a commoner of Piacenza (1387), we find a *guarnaccone* (a type of

8.

12

9.

heavy cape) of blue camlet, with pearl *pomelli* (round apple-shaped buttons).

We read of a Florentine lawyer rebuking a lady for wearing a number of buttons greater than that allowed. She replied, in strict logic, that they had no shanks and that, in addition, there were no buttonholes, so that what she was wearing came under the heading of lawful ornaments.

This was still possible in the 15th century, because fastenings for clothes, although fairly rare, took the form of hooks and eyes bought at the goldsmiths.

8. Turkish style dress with huge turban. *Libro del Sarto,* repertorio n.54. Venice, *Fondazione Querini Stampalia.*

9. Pear- and apple-shaped buttons for "Gaillarde" dancers. N.Carosio. *Il Ballerino.*

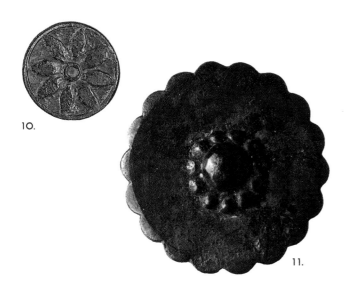

11.

10. Bronze buttons with stylized floral decoration.17th century.

11. At the end of the 17th century, everyday buttons were still made of iron.

14

The Renaissance shed the refiniment and elegance of its courts and artists on buttons as well. Antiquity-mania led to a flowering of splendid geometrical forms, and buttons quickly moved away from utility to luxury, until they became veritable pieces of solid gold and silver jewellery, studded with precious stones. A mantle said to have been designed by the very elegant Marchioness of Mantua, Isabella d'Este, included more than twenty most valuable buttons as pure ornament. The chronicles relate that Vallonico, Prince and Duke of Savoy, wore in Venice, on his return from Hungary, a rich collar "of the finest leather, buttoned in front with gold buttons", which obviously did not pass unnoticed.

The 16th century saw the development of the art of enamelling applied to buttons; it seems that Francis I of France owned and wore the first *parures* that appeared on the market. In 1566, his grandson Charles IX laid down regulations for the work of button-enamellers, and his brother, Henry III, made laws in April 1583 for the manufacture and use of enamel, glass and crystal buttons.

Accordingly, the custom of loading fifteenth century marriageable daughters with jewellery to make them more showy and attractive now only allowed them to wear chains and collars, and carry rosaries of gold and garnet beads, but enamel ornaments were forbidden.

Queen Elizabeth I of England favoured buttons for military uniforms, deciding that metal ones should be sewn all around the cuffs of the soldiers' coats to break them of the beastly habit of wiping their noses on their sleeves.

In the 16th century, *péroli* were mainly worn on mens' coats; their were still the work of goldsmiths, and still subject to repressive measures. The Venetian *Magistrato delle Pompe* decided, on 20 August 1644, that "the aforesaid clothes shall all be close-fitting and there must be no gold buttons on the sleeves". The inventories of the time are full of buttons, and in 1680 buttons and buttonholes finally came together for fastening clothes, losing their mainly ornamental role. Jewelled buttons were still made by goldsmiths, but by now there were buttons of crystal and mother-of-pearl, mounted on silver or silvered copper, which were more hard-wearing than gold.

However, the precious-metal buttons adorning mens' clothes in Baroque time represented an investment they carried with them in cases of emergency. Captain Kidd, the famous pirate, always wore nothing but gold buttons, and his adventurous English and French filibustering colleagues did likewise while chasing Spanish galleons on the way to the Indies. Buttons, therefore, made the rich man, and it was believed at the time that someone whose clothes bore twenty gold and sixty silver buttons (sic!) could never go bankrupt- at least not until he had been shorn by a rogue with a razor specializing in button-theft.

At the time we are dealing with, buttons were not sewn on with thread; once the shank had been put through the appropriate hole, the button was secured with a metal strip. In this way the same set of buttons could be used for different coats. Seventeenth-century mens' coats grew longer during the last quarter of the period, with rich ornamental buttoning, and shorter and wider sleeves showed off the white lace cuffs of the shirt at the wrist. The sleeves were decorated with high cuffs, ornate with braid and buttons.

Metal buttons acquired great importance, value apart, when they began

12.

12. Portrait of Francis 1st of Este. Guercino. 1630. Geneva, Revillot collection.

to appear on the uniforms of the military orders and armies organized in the late 16th century. For this purpose, makers supplied buttons of iron, brass, copper, tin and pewter, an alloy of copper and zinc.

ELEGANCE AND REFINIMENT FOR DANDIES

Throughout the "century of enlightenment", masculine elegance depended upon pretty stuffs, lace and jabots, and decorative buttons played a part in this search for refiniment.

The many-buttoned surtout was the standard dress. Until 1730 its shape remained almost unchanged: full and long-reaching to the calf, it had square skirts back and front and a single opening with a row of precious-metal buttons down to the knee, with matching buttonholes that were never used. Sleeves were rather short, opening out a little at the wrist, with high cuffs fastened to the rest of the sleeve with buttons: pockets, before and behind, were horizontal, with shaped flaps and buttons, of course.

Gentlemen wishing to appear elegant were advised that "the coat should have no buttonholes, except for the two nearest the collar, in which one may insert a carnation at least as big as a sunflower". But perhaps the garment of greatest interest to the dandies of the Rococo was the waistcoat or *camisiola*, as it was known in Venice. In the winter of 1787 the waistcoat began to invade even the French provinces, where its arrival had been announced by the society columns of Paris newspapers. The dandy had to possess dozens, perhaps hundreds of them, magnificently embroidered with hunting scenes, chivalrous duels and even naval battles. The waistcoat, contrasting in colour with the coat itself, was made of fine material (silk-satin, velvet or mohair) and bore conspicuous copper buttons, which in this case were always fastened.

Since its appearance on the male fashion scene as a coloured asterisk and catalyzer of refined taste, the waistcoat has lived a life of its own, independently of the rest of the costume. This is also true of its buttons, which were not necessarily matched to those of the coat with which it

13. Metal button with relief. Late 18th century.

14. Enamelled metal button. Slight floral motif with gilt metal surround. France, 18th century. Corinaldi-Bomisa Collection.

13.

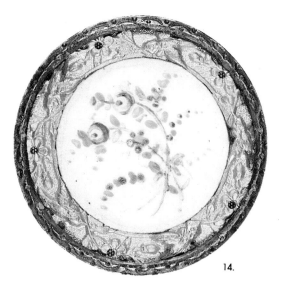

14.

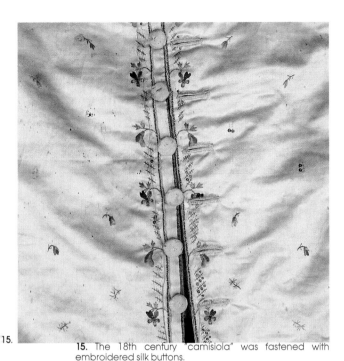

15. The 18th century "camisiola" was fastened with embroidered silk buttons.

16. The embroidered tail-coat worn by young 18th century dandies bore flat buttons with floral motifs in silver.

was worn, but were more valuable, or at least more original, following the fancies of 18th century button-craftsmen.

Buttons bore pictures of animals, bouquets of flowers, the Twelve Caesars, the King of France, a different letter for each button making up the name of the loved one or her portrait in miniature. These were transferred to the discs in various ways: sculpted on ivory, fixed with different-coloured enamels, made of tiny mosaic fragments, painted as miniatures or drawn in sepia. And even though Mr Strasser had invented an almost perfect imitation diamond that bore his name, between 1774 and 1791 "three thousand five hundred and thirty-six medium and small diamonds were purchased to provide buttons and for decorating the King's sword-hilt".(Bion: *Inventaire des diamants de la couronne*, 1791). In England, Wedgwood produced famous and beautiful white porcelain cameos on a light-blue ground, set in gold and crystal.

The 18th century was also the golden age of frogging, a sort of silk-cord trimming, usually black or gold, which joined two similar buttons. These were originally known as brandenburgs, appearing as they did for the first time on military uniforms in Brandeburg at the end of the 17th century. Haberdashers

17. A glassed water-colour landscape in a copper surround forms an elegant coat-button of the mid-18th century.

18. Embroidered silk button. Italy 18th century.

18.

19.

INDUSTRIAL INTERESTS

From the late 17th century onwards the button began its timid march towards industrial production. Buttons of precious stones or metals, or of embroidered silk, the unrivalled inheritance of artisanal skill, were existing side by side with other types that could be mass-produced. The phenomenon became quite evident in the 18th century, and grew steadily thanks to a new philosophy of clothes that was not concerned with outer garments alone, but included undergarments for men, women and children.

The production of simple concave bone buttons began in the 12th century and was never superseded. They were especially used for men's shirts and drawers. Millions of buttons with five holes, four on the edges and one in the centre, separate the underwear-buttons of the 18th century from thousands of millions of similar, but four-holed ones, produced from the 19th century onwards. The producing area for five- and four-holed bone buttons was the French town of Meru and its outskirts along the Loire valley.

As an historical approach, it is interesting to analyse the various materials used in button-manufacture and their appearance on the scene. This is really a history of technology; after the middle of the 18th century, buttons form part of contemporary protoindustrial culture.

20.

began to make them, ornamenting them with slivers of crystal in certain cases. They changed their name to frogs, and were much in fashion during the 20's and 30's of the 19th century, both for men and women, and held the front of their overcoats closed against the wintry blasts. They were later to be seen mainly on men's smoking-jackets, but became fashionable again in the very late 1880's on evening mantles and boleros, for sportswear on coats and on sheepskin jackets.

19. Two China Wedgwood buttons with copper surrounds. England, late 18th early 19th century.

20. Link buttons for a sumptuous tail-coat, painted on glass, strass surround and silvered-metal backing. France, last quarter 18th century.

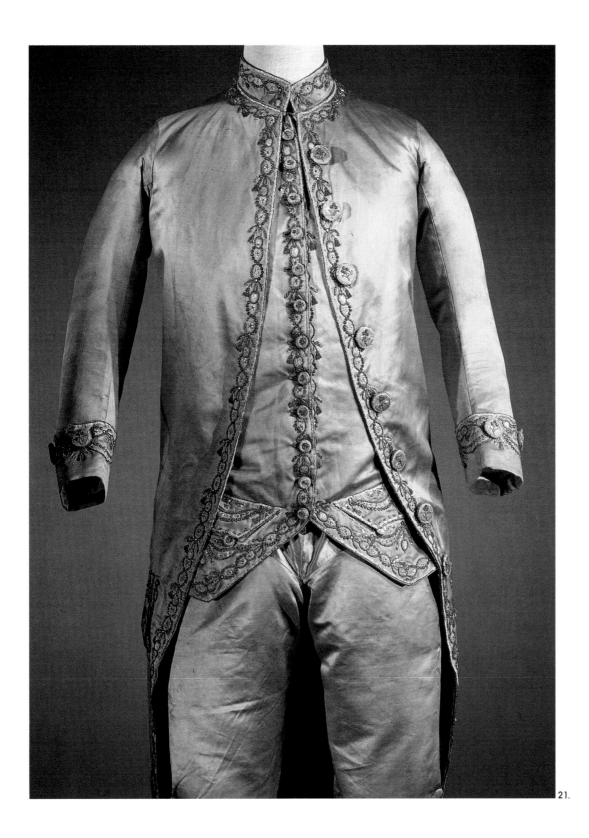

21.

21. Men's clothes in the third quarter of the 18th century had embroidered silk matching buttons on the coat, waistcoat and trouserlegs.

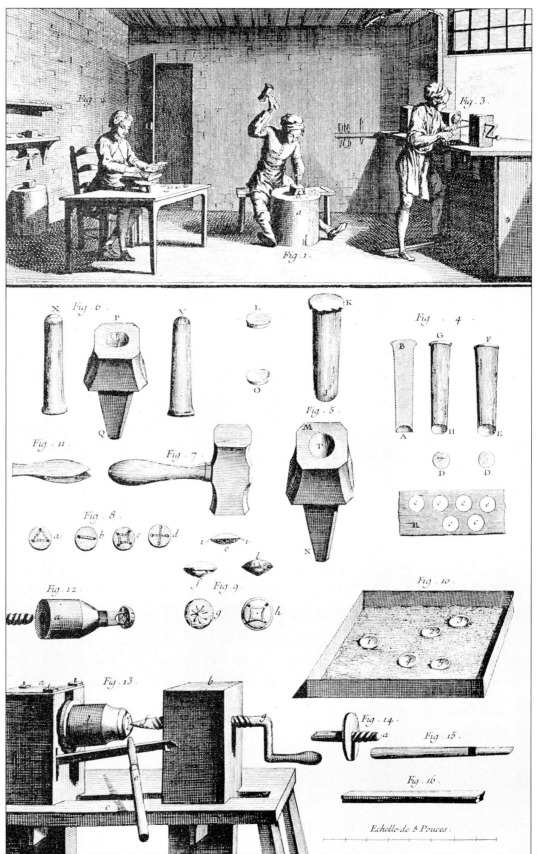

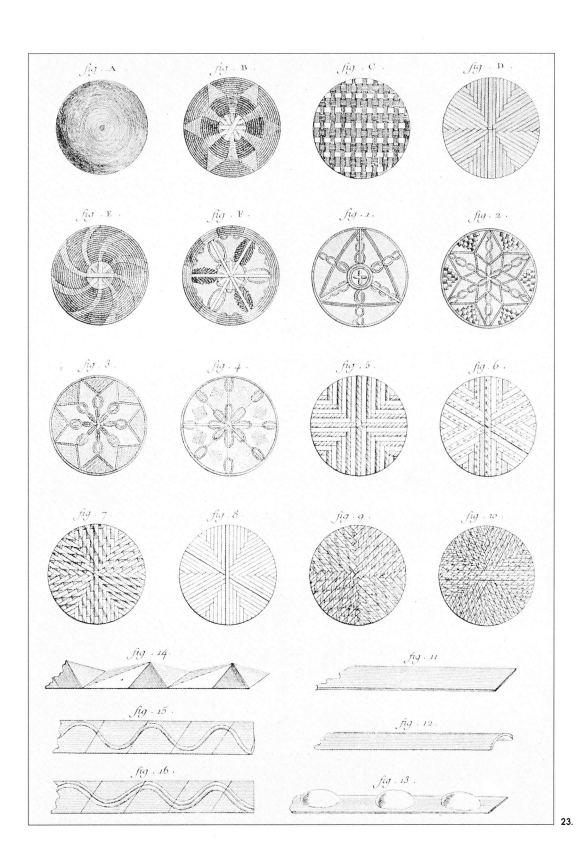

23.

22.23. Plates in the *Encyclopédie* show the protoindustrial manufacture of metal buttons, which flourished at the time in France and England, and designs for embroidered buttons woven by the skilful hands of the *boutonniers passamentiers.*

24.

25.

Several companies were established in England, which recruited craftsmen for manufacturing uniform-buttons. Patents were taken out in Birmingham between 1770 and 1793 for the decoration and finishing of metal buttons, and the city became a centre for such operations, finally becoming the Button Capital, especially once Matthew Boulton had perfected a system for making steel bezels for valuable, and even for enamelled buttons.

The English manufacturers were particularly interested in flat shiny steel buttons, 35 mm in diameter, which shone like mirrors. These were made of tiny plates of metal, arranged in star or lozenge-patterns on an opaque ground. Others were hammered into cabochons or flower-patterns. Shiny buttons were a godsend to certain gamesters, if we are to believe Baron de Frénilly, who was especially welcome at the house of an impoverished French provincial family of title. "Whenever I was invited to their house, I always lost at cards. It was fashionable then to wear big smooth buttons which reflected beautifully. Mine reflected the cards I held, and my hosts found them the height of fashion". Once the Baron changed his steel buttons for cloth-covered ones, he may have seemed less elegant, and the games of bezique came to an end.

Steel was not the only metal used in place of gold and silver: there was pinchbeck, an alloy of copper, brass and zinc, invented by and named after the English watchmaker Christopher Pinchbeck, and nickel silver also. Metal buttons, flat at first and convex later, all with the usual shank behind, bore in the 19th century coats of arms, monograms, symbols of associations and confraternities and the badges of regiments, which were beginning to appear in various European armies.

A new natural material reached the market in the 1830's - vegetable ivory, known in its countries of origin as *corozo* or *tagua*. It is the hard dense albumen of the nut of certain tropical palm trees, shipped as ballast in sailing-vessels from Panama and Ecuador to Europe, where at first it only encumbered the wharves of Hamburg. Sacks of this "ballast" were then sent up river, and the *Steinnüsse* (stone nuts), as they where called in Germany, ended up in Bohemian towns that vied with England and France in the European button-market. The consistency of this substance, very like elephant-ivory, and its ease of working opened the corozo era in 1867. The manufacture of buttons from vegetable ivory long remained a German staple of trade. In the Bergamo region of Italy, where button-making was concentrated, the firm *Tacchini & Fanti* was already making corozo buttons in 1869. Some twenty years later, when *Tacchini & Fanti* merged with the *Società Anonima Manifattura Bottoni*, production began on an industrial scale, the name of corozo was Italianized as *bottoni di frutto* and, at the Paris Exhibition of 1900, the firm won a gold medal for button-merit.

23

24.25. At the end of the 18th century, army uniforms were covered in buttons, with different symbols for each regiment. Here we have Grenadiers, Austrian mountain troops and Spanish Cavalry. G. Ferrario *op. cit.*

26. A pot-pourri of the 18th century buttons: silver with insert of engraved silver strips; decorated with golden sequins; bronze with insert of mirror-glass and engraved silver; silver and silver-gilt repoissé laminated, engraved and satined in concentric circles on a bone core. Italy, France.

26.

THE EIGHTEEN-HUNDREDS, A BUTTONED-UP CENTURY

A type of artisanal button much used in the 18th century had been that of a glass dome in a copper surround, silvered in cases of greater elegance, under which were placed bits of coloured feathers, dried rose-leaves or tiny prints bearing a rebus that told of romance. The latter were peremptorily replaced at the outbreak of the French Revolution by themes from the new order, ranging from the outline of the Bastille to portraits of the heroes of the day, Caps of Liberty, the March of the women on Versailles, tricolour cockades or a few bars of the *Marseillaise*. Epic mottoes like *Vivre libre ou mourir* were engraved in relief on steel buttons (made in France) or on the more plebeian iron ones worn by the sanculottes.

The mania for "symbolic" buttons was not confined to dandies striving for originality or to militant partisans, for it

28.

24

27. Ladies wore buttons on riding-habits only, which were fastened with silver buttons in Louis XV's age. P.L. de Giaferri, *L'Histoire du Costume Féminin Français.*

27.

began just before the Revolution and continued long after it. A taste for buttons survived the 18th century owing to two parallel factors, according to Nicole Pellegrin in her book *Les Vêtements de la Liberté*: on the one hand, the attainment, or wish to attain, to appearances of ease and power on the part of a large section of the Third Estate, and, on the other, the spread of a middle-class style of dress, austere and without adornment. Fancy buttons, like ties and waistcoats, conferred a certain individuality on costumes that were both socially and sexually neuter, and made it possible discreetly to follow the fashion. And since, apart from womens' riding-habits, female dress at this time was completely devoid of buttons, these ornate little discs are often fingered by gentlemen in contemporary portraits, as though they were using that gesture to transmit an image of power to posterity.

28. Gilt metal for tail-coats and similar wear at the end of the 18th and early 19th centuries, solid and incised, or worked in the typical English buttons methodology.

Indeed, continues the author, where would Napoleon be without his waistcoat-buttons? A Bonaparte who didn't know where to put his hands.

The situation remained stable in the early years of the 19th century, and some decades were to pass before signs of innovation could appear. But something always has to catch the eye, and certain aesthetic concessions were made by varying the number of buttons or by preferring the glint of metal to the more traditional "camouflaged" button, covered with the same cloth as the frock-coat, or made of black embroidered cord.

In 1844, a certain clever Frenchman, Monsieur Parent, invented a new type of shank for buttons, which could now be attached to the garment without the need for the usual holes. This was a small but important discovery with regard to future developments.

29. On men's tail-coats the prevailing fashion was for metal buttons, sometimes in two rows. *Petit Courrier des Dames* 1822. *Costume collection*, Venice, Palazzo Mocenigo.

30. At the beginning of the 19th century, buttons were fanciful and valuable; the water colour lion under glass with a copper surround, of English manufacture; the fly is in semi-precious stone. The beetle, of very fine French workmanship, is in mosaic; the dove is painted on china, and the miniatures are on ivory with silvered metal surround.

30.

29.

two or three holes for expensive shirts, or of natural-coloured bone for those worn by simpler people. Early 19th century evening-dress was made up in dark bronze, dark blue or bottle-green cloth with two rows of buttons, either of matching colours or of shiny metal.

1846 fashion dictated evening waistcoats either of black satin with jet buttons or of smooth white cashmere with little shiny convex gold buttons, set very close together. For summer wear the fashionable cloth was white piqué with mother-of-pearl buttons.

In the very middle of the century -1856- there appeared a garment that was to cause a revolution in male costume: the tailless sack-jacket. The line was straight and short, accentuated by doing up the first two buttons only of the single-breasted front. This innovation slowly replaced the long tail-coat fastened with three buttons made of silk needlework or crochet, especially at the end of the

In case of masculine elegance, the use of buttons for shirt-fronts followed the disappearence of the jabot, and these could be seen in so far as the wide silk neckcloth permitted. In principle, the shirt had five small flat or concave buttons, always white and of mother-of-pearl with

31. The buttons on the uniform of a civilian Papal functionary in the early 18th century are of convex silver, engraved with the pontifical arms.

32. Livery buttons, flat in the 18th and convex in the 19th centuries, are usually made of silver or burnished metal. The back has a ring for inserting a little chain.

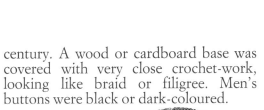

century. A wood or cardboard base was covered with very close crochet-work, looking like braid or filigree. Men's buttons were black or dark-coloured.

33. Buttons with hunting or riding motif were very frequent in the second half of the 19th century. Water-colour miniatures under glass, with a copper surround; enamel dog on a blue ground and a beagle incised on crystal. A butterfly painted on black glass. France, last quarter of 19th century.

34. Buttons with animal subjects in colour combinations of two metals; brass and facetted steel. Late 19th and early 20th centuries. Corinaldi-Bomisa Collection.

35. The *Giornale dei Sarti*, August 1853. Venice, *Palazzo Mocenigo*.

35.

FOR LADIES TOO, AT LAST!

With very few exceptions, the history of buttons long remained a masculine preserve, and men were the users of two thirds of the world production of buttons until the mid-19th century, displaying, showing them off and even wasting them. But at about that time the advent of French *haute couture*, coming after the rise and fall of the crinoline, meant that women's clothes also began to be decorated, rather than merely fastened, with the object that had, from earliest times, been defined as of less value than the smallest farthing.

36. Very fine late 19th century tortoise-shell buttons delicately worked with incrustations of mother-of-pearl, crystal and precious metals. France, second half of the 19th century.

37. Factories were set up in the 19th century at Gablons in Bohemia for manufacturing buttons made of jet, strass and glass paste.

The revenge of the button seems to have been exuberant to judge from the sarcastic comments of a contemporary fashion-reporter: "In the summer of 1877 ladies seem to have been attacked by button-madness". Their dresses, especially in their upper parts, were inundated with buttons most of them made of metal. The writer asks whether these button-maniacs were suffering from a cleanliness-syndrome, as the metal buttons of the time, especially the gilt ones, had to be polished frequently to appear in all their glory.

Ladies' buttons were covered in the same material as the dress, or in silk trimming, often of the same shade as the dress itself.

Trimming-buttons derive from the elaborate embroidery-techniques of the 17th and 18th centuries, used to decorate the jackets and frock-coats of Italian, French and Spanish noblemen. These, however, were made of gold or silver thread, incorporating fragments of precious stones or crystal, whereas late 19th century buttons were made of shiny silk cord, so woven as to form a low-relief design. The gem-fragments were replaced by coloured beads or bits of jet, a compact black brilliant form of lignite found all over Europe, from the Rhone estuary to the Pyrenees, and from Sicily to Saxony and Prussia. Morning or "calling" dresses often took the form of long, close-fitting jackets with rows of little cloth-covered buttons of a darker or contrasting shade. Their ornamental aspect is evident, even though they have a functional role also. By the end of the 19th century their buttonholes are embroidered in festoon stitch, called buttonhole stitch in this context, and the garment almost always fastens centrally, with an occasional slight leftward displacement. Indeed, in the matter of buttoning, it was decided to mark the difference between the sexes:

36.

37.

men always had to have their right hand free, so that men's clothes still button on the right in order to make things easier for the left hand, while women's weapon-free hand can button from right to left. This positioning came in during the last quarter of the 19th century, when buttons became a visible part of feminine costume.

Buttons also began to appear on nightdresses, which at first had three buttonholes, although more fully-draped ones were preferred later, fastened with a single button. The *jupon* or underskirt essential for the set of the dress, which had to fall impeccably when descending in flounces, cascades and bows from the *tournure*, was fastened behind with a button, flat of course and covered in white material.

When Queen Victoria became a widow in 1861 and laid down rules of mourning, opaque black buttons, or shiny jet ones found their place on all types of widow's weeds. Naturally, the Queen's buttons were made of real jet, but the million of shiny mourning buttons that then appeared on dresses of solemn black were often made of glass, embroidery or cloth. Jet and black glass buttons began to be made in the 19th century at Gablons, in Bohemia, site of the biggest glass-button factories. As time went by, Austria took over pride of place in this trade until, in the 20th century, there was a great falling off in demand and this type of button gave place to those made of synthetics -more easily worked and, above all, cheaper.

Very often, too, little buttons for boots, with a metal shank, were of shiny black, and were made in France from papier maché, waterproofed in a oil bath and then enamel-painted. As the shank was short and leather buttonholes difficult to penetrate, ladies of the time did up their boots with a buttonhook, which always

29

38. Opaque jet buttons, with metal and mirror glass inserts, in burnished silver. The black ones are meant for full mourning, the others for half-mourning.

39. Mourning-wear. *La Mode Illustrée*, July 1914.

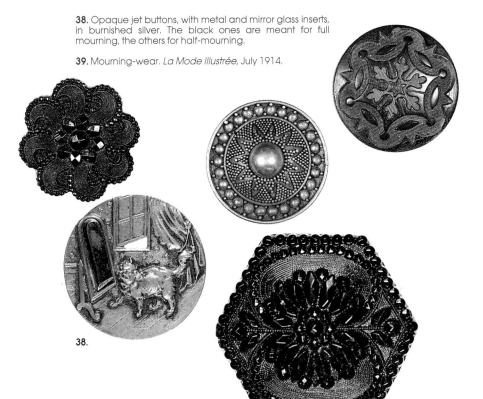

38.

39.

40. Button-mania exploded in the last quarter of the 19th century, and even extended to little girl's dresses. *Il Bazar*, November 1876.

formed part of the silver or tortoise-shell requisites, each bearing a monogram, that went with a bridal trousseau and were laid out carefully on the dressing-table, that stood in the bedrooms of even the least demanding women.

Buttonhooks were also used to do up gloves, especially the long ones with a small vertical opening at the wrist, fastened by one or two, or as many as five, flat or rounded pearl-shaped buttons. Doing up the right hand glove led to certain contortions, but a little practice soon put matters right.

The rest of the story belongs to a new century.

MORE RECENT HISTORY: THE TWENTIETH CENTURY

41.

MORE ESSENTIAL THAN EVER

In rhythm with the new century, the smart woman's wardrobe acquires new types of garment, dictated by the requirements of fashion - especially as seen from Paris - but also by needs which are slowly making their appearence. Trends, of course, do not necessarily follow the calendar, but suggestions in the most widely-read reviews for women regarding a freer concept of movement, coupled with a wish to imitate philosophies of dress mainly inspired by the other side of the English Channel, combine to suggest a new style of living. In the first years of the 20th century women began to walk about in town, to go out shopping in the morning, or visit their dressmakers'. The most emancipated among them - mainly American or North European women -

were leaving their houses for office-work, which they had attained to by breaking through the delaying tactics and powerful taboos of contemporary society. Women and girls soon began to wear tailor-mades (coat and skirt), the feminine version of men's clothing. Their jackets were fastened with every kind of fancy button: horn tortoise-shell and metal. For the earliest summer tailor-mades there were haberdashery buttons in white or *écru*.

41. Sparkling marcassite buttons, to be added to clothes at the appropriate moment, were afterwards kept in special boxes. Italy, c. 1900.

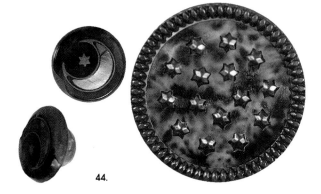

44.

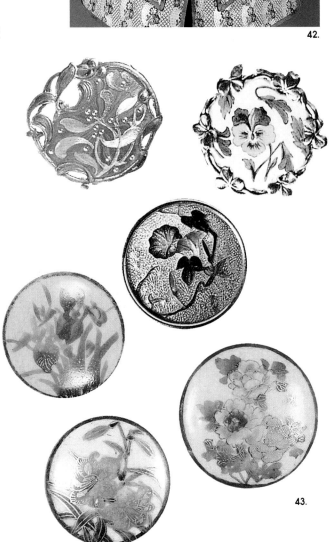

42.

Buttons were medium-sized or large, in one or two rows, always opposite buttonholes even where these were fake and the buttons only there to heighten the line of the skirt, which often had a straight, narrow flare in front. The coat and skirt were completed by the blouse, which always buttoned even if the little fabric-covered, needlework, crochet or mother-of-pearl buttons could only be seen through the pleats of the full Belle Epoque/Art Nouveau jabot. Cloaks were still long, but they formed part of the trend toward innovation. Double-breasted *redingotes* were also worn, with huge lapels suggestive of shoulder-capes. Dust-coats were essential for the privileged and daring ladies who could go joy-riding in motor-cars with a "sport" of a husband at the wheel. These coats were waisted or sack-shaped, often double-breasted, and fastened with showy flat mother-of-pearl, crystal or tortoise-shell buttons. Collars were masculine in cut and the sleeves turned back. Hats were covered in thick veiling to preserve delicate pink complexions from damage by the dust raised at breathtaking speed.

42. Ladies' double-breasted waistcoats. The buttons are covered in the same silk material. c.1905.

43. A series of valuable enamel buttons of French and English manufacture, generally worn with ladies' elegant dress and waistcoats. Three wonderful Japanese *satsuma* examples hand-painted on china (1830). This type of decoration influenced the *art nouveau* buttons popular in the first decade of the 19th century.

44. Celluloid buttons, some with metal or mother-of-pearl decoration, for suits, dust-coats and sportswear worn by ladies at the beginning of the 19th century.

43.

45.

45. Suits make a triumphal entry into women's 19th century wardrobes and are destined to remain irreplaceable thereafter. Very often the buttons are showy, as in this case. *La Saison*, April 1899.

Mother-of-pearl or tortoise-shell buttons were often replaced by large white, transparent or coloured celluloid ones, especially on sportswear. Celluloid was the first man-made substance, widely used in button-manufacture. Invented as an imitation of ivory by John Hyatt of New Jersey in 1869, it was originally used for making billiard-balls. Ivory-coloured celluloid, or that mixed with spangles or metal filings, formed buttons with ornate shanks of late 18th century style. At the

beginning of the 20th century, thanks to new manufacturing processes, coloured celluloid was all the rage until, because of its high inflammability, it gave way to less dangerous substances that were all more attractive because of their ...novelty.

For more formal wear, ladies used fewer, but far more visible buttons, especially gold or silver ones decorated with transparent sepia enamel and a light floral motif surrounded by little facetted diamonds. These were created by Fabergé, a famous Russian goldsmith of French extraction, who rose to fame at the Paris Universal Exhibition of 1900, with technical eclecticism, new decorative motifs and the vaporous styles of the *Belle Epoque*.

Meanwhile, in tune with Lalique's refined glassware, the more accessible button was adorned with the profiles of women with huge heads of hair, or "floral" and "dragon-fly" women in the flexible poses dear to Art Nouveau. The early 20th century witnessed the reappearance of buttons made of marcassite, a derivation of pyrites crystal, especially for wear with silk, velvet or dark moiré dresses; and also of strass, which the times were reviving almost two centuries after the invention of this imitation diamond by Mr Strasser who gave it his name. Strass was almost always used to decorate the framework of buttons or covered, like a carpet or a mosaic, the surface of various materials into which it was inserted, or merely glued. Strass buttons of the *Belle Epoque* were worn on the evening gowns of beautiful, elegant women, and those who were "too" beautiful or "too" generous, in the eyes of current respectability, and who heightened the appeal of their *toilettes mondaines* with "brilliant" buttons. Strass buttons, also known as rhinestones, were made into buckles in imitation of those of the 18th century. These were of the greatest effect on wide, draped black satin belts. At the beginning of the century valuable buttons, like those of marcassite, glass or enamel, did not come with the dress, but were bought separately and kept in special boxes, and then sewn onto dresses when the occasion arose, whether dictated by fashion or fancy.

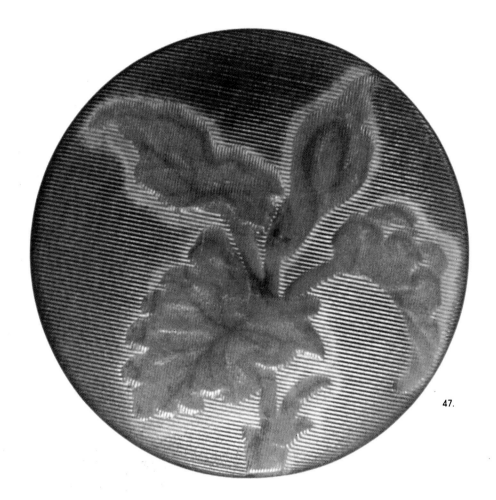

47.

CHRONICLES OF ELEGANCE

The *Ville Lumière* and its *couturiers* became increasingly famous and important as the carefree *Belle Epoque* continued. Their splendid dress-houses, temples of the cult of elegance, were besieged by women of the brilliant society that had chosen Paris as their fashionable headquarters. The Caillot sisters, Lanvin and Poiret were at the height of their careers, and laid down a law which brooked no discussion on matters of women's dress.

At the height of the enthusiasm provoked in 1911 by the Russian ballet season, with Lifar as its leading dancer, Poiret introduced exoticism into the fashion of the day. As his talent fluctuated this way and that, there appeared, among other things, asymetrical buttonings for jackets and blouses, pushed over to the left shoulder in imitation of the typical "Russian" tunics worn by the dancers. Button-decoration ranged from Russian to African styles. There was a return to the past in the frequent use of Assyrian lion's-heads and Renaissance motifs. However, the strongest influence at the beginning of the century was that of Japanese art, which affected all art-forms, and especially the applied arts: the whole Art Nouveau movement is impregnated with suggestions from Oriental thought and taste.

Gilt flowers and birds in high relief on black ebony grounds, engraved with great refinement, alternate with birds of Paradise and ibises, tufts of leaves falling against misty backgrounds, and chrysanthemums with graciously curving petals.

46. Visiting outfit with marcassite buttons. *Les Modes*, 1908.

47. Very elegant celluloid button decorated with an *art nouveau* motif. France, c. 1900.

In an article appearing in *La Mode Illustrée* of 31 December 1911, we read: "Great quantities of buttons, of all shapes and sizes, from the little ones on priest's cassocks to discs 7 cm in diameter. Many dresses are buttoned all the way down, in front or at the side, straight or at angle. Buttons often match the colour of the dress or are covered in the same materials; at other times they are covered in different material of contrasting colours, or are chosen from the innumerable models of *haute fantaisie*. The latest novelty is said to be concave crystal buttons, those of "antique" engraved silver, others entirely of strass, and little flat, concave or ball-shaped mother-of-pearl buttons. Huge blond or tabby tortoise-shell buttons were selling for 30 francs a dozen! There were also *gallinite* buttons, of a composition that could be coloured or marbled. It was made from hardened casein, collected from the "dairy factories" of the Argentine State, dried and exported to French manufacturers, who made it into something looking like agate, the singular origin of which could only be guessed at by a magician.

36

49.

48.

48. Gilt metal buttons with strass in the most typical style of the period. France, early 19th century.

49. At the beginning of the century there was a vogue for braided buttons, sometimes coloured and brightened up with gold or silver thread, as dictated by Poiret.

50. Metal buttons, incised, painted and enamelled, or in combination with various materials as base (fabric, mother-of-pearl, mirror-glass, glass paste) were much in evidence on overcoats and "walking costumes". At the beginning of the 20th century filigree metal buttons began to appear. Collections Corinaldi-Bomisa and R. Goni.

50.

51. All the flimsy summer dresses of the 1908-9 seasons bore fabric, coloured celluloid or metal buttons. *La Mode Parisienne.*

51.

FASHION MAGAZINES

Suggestion from culture of the eighteenth and nineteenth centuries influenced, during the 1910's, both manners and fashion in high society. Magazine headings that a century earlier had "instructed women" in the fashions of the time made their reappearance; in June 1912 the *Journal des Dames et des Modes* reappeared with a facsimile of its issue of a hundred years before.

Every fortnight for two years -it was to suspend publication on the outbreak of war in August 1914 - the paper provided its chosen readership with accounts of smart Parisian events, plays and fashion, with accompanying illustrations. News-items went into the slightest details of clothing, including accessories, ornaments and buttons, and only rarely did its columns deal with matters of male attire, which in those days was, by definition, sober, elegant and unchangeable.

Truly elegant women, said the journal in autumn 1912, were trying to copy the Persian style, suggested by the Oriental fantasies of Poiret, and also styles of the 18th century, the *fourreau* and drapery. Dresses were very loose and draped, in soft fabrics, and worn with very close-fitting, completely buttoned waistcoats, often of heavy damask or embroidered satin, in bright colours, cut from the "undercoat" of a masher of the Watteau era or, worse still, from an ancient chasuble. Sacrilege!, and even double sacrilege, said the writer of the article, for ladies did not hesitate to insert strass, crystal, agate, cornelian or sculpted bone buttons into these precious materials, recreating the ornamental function of the eighteenth century dandy's buttons. Other, less iconoclastic waistcoats, with

40

52.

53.

54.

52. *Lingerie* summer wear fastened with link-buttons of white braid. *La Mode Illustrée* 1909.

53. Pink cloth suit fastened with four big self-coloured buttons. *La Mode Illustrée* 1909.

54. Braided or cloth-covered buttons, with their buttonholes in yellow silk thread, are only there for decoration. The use of silk buttonholes in contrasting colours was known as *à la milanaise*.

shawl collars, bore metal buttons along the whole opening. The deathless sculpted mother-of- pearl buttons, sometimes in the form of a cameo or outlined in black, was of large dimensions and used for fastening cloaks. The same article revealed that new jackets for women were similar in form to men's dinner-jackets, with rounded lapels joined at the waist by link-buttons of silk cord. Straight collars, little black neckties and enamel buttons on the ruched front of the white silk blouses completed the outfit - rather austere, but suitable for afternoon visits.

For the summer, however, a freer style was allowed, thanks to technology, which had found an alternative to celluloid in bakelite, the invention of Leo Hendrick Baekeland, a Belgian living in America. The most popular bakelite buttons were shaped like fruit, to decorate and fasten with rows of nuts, little apples, strawberries or cherries the white jackets known as *lingerie*, because they were made

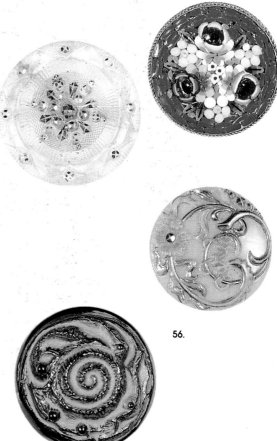

56.

55.

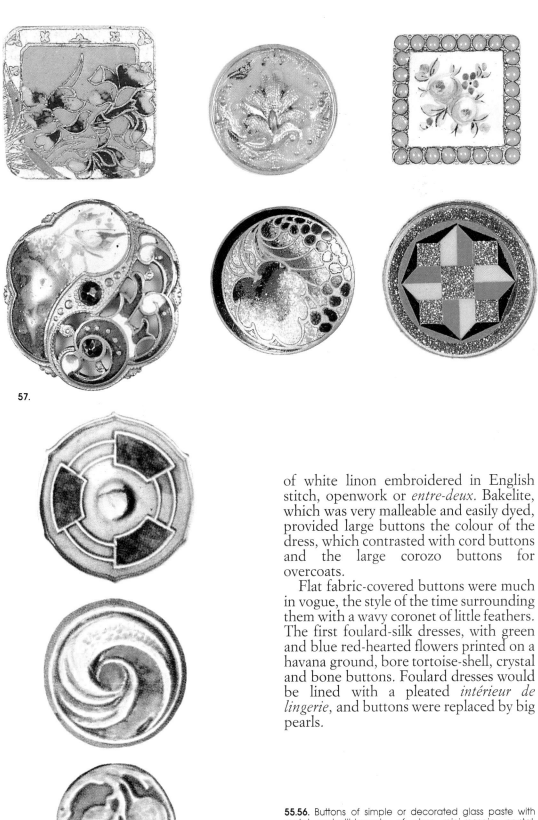

57.

of white linon embroidered in English stitch, openwork or *entre-deux*. Bakelite, which was very malleable and easily dyed, provided large buttons the colour of the dress, which contrasted with cord buttons and the large corozo buttons for overcoats.

Flat fabric-covered buttons were much in vogue, the style of the time surrounding them with a wavy coronet of little feathers. The first foulard-silk dresses, with green and blue red-hearted flowers printed on a havana ground, bore tortoise-shell, crystal and bone buttons. Foulard dresses would be lined with a pleated *intérieur de lingerie*, and buttons were replaced by big pearls.

55.56. Buttons of simple or decorated glass paste with metal embellishments, of glass mini-mosaic, crystal, precious stones and minerals (cupralite and marcassite) on elegant ladies' dresses of the 1900's.

57.58. French and English enamel buttons of the early 1900's bear designs in *Art Nouveau* taste. The three buttons of greeny-blue enamel were sold by Liberty's of London. *The Liberty Style.*

58.

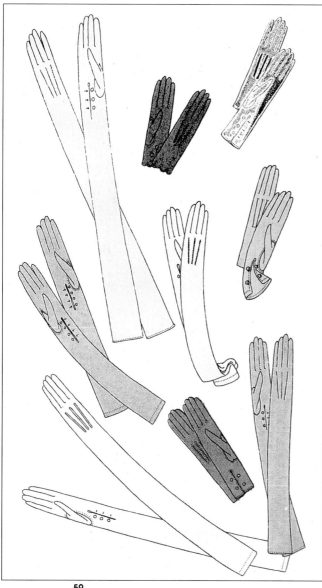

59.

60.

59. *Le Journal des Dames et des Modes* shows the latest thing in gloves; gloves-lengths were measured at the time in "little buttons": one for short gloves, up to eleven or thirteen of them for long gloves covering the whole arm. 1913.

60. Three metal buttons, enamelled and lithographed, for Belle Epoque buttonholes. England, c.1910.

61. Tin buttons on sportswear survived the First World War.

62. Tin buttons. Italy, first quarter 20th century.

63. A military- inspired suit with metal buttons, designed by Dudovich for *La Donna* in 1919. G. Butazzi, *Moda Arte Storia e Società.*

In 1914, at the beginning of the catastrophe that was to change their vision of the world for countless inhabitants of our planet, there were attractive novelties forthcoming in the field of button-fashion: a profusion of olive or acorn-shaped buttons, and balls of jade or bone, in striking contrast to the sobriety of the costume, fastened the three-quarter-length jackets of loose-fitting striped tailor-mades, worn with boots that had black velvet uppers and antilope heels, the buttons of which had a black velvet shank.

While on the subject of *Belle Epoque* fashion accessories, gloves must not be forgotten. They were absolutely indispensable in the early 1910's. Short, half length, long or elbow-length ladies'

gloves were generally made of *suède* in three colours only -white, pearl- grey and champagne. They were worn with every kind of outfit, even the less elegant ones, and followed precise rules. The opening was usually provided with three iridescent pearl-shaped button, and the gloves were never removed, nor the buttons undone. In those days men still bent over to kiss gallantly a well-gloved hand, smiling with all their teeth as they did so.

61.

62.

63.

64.

MEN, ON THE OTHER HAND...

In 1913 *La Mode Nouvelle* launched the idea of offering buttons as a present to well-dressed men for their impeccable shirts. White pearl, it suggested, was preferred to black, the fashion for which was dying out. Pearl-shaped buttons were very popular, whatever their material - porcelain, wood, glass, jet or real pearls- or form: round, tubular, cabochon, regular or baroque pearls.

There were also mother-of-pearl buttons set in gold, and diamond or ruby ones (for those who could afford so expensive a present). Cameos and simple gold buttons were reserved for men of a certain age.

Young men certainly preferred mother-of-pearl with enamel, or with silver, gold olive-shaped, or red and blue enamel buttons to go with their shirts for elegant daytime wear. The *Journal des Dames et des Modes* of 1 October 1912 says that with the new tails to make the wearer look like prince Metternich as a young man and

64. A much-appreciated gift: a set of buttons by the famous Franco-Russian jeweller Fabergé, who specialized in beautiful enamelling on gold, mother-of-pearl with gold surrounds, olive-shape (Corinaldi-Bomisa Collection) or *solitaire* buttons of eccentric style in gold and enamel for boiled-shirts fronts (R. Goni Collection).

65. The midnight-blue tail-coat designed by Krieck, the English tailor, as illustrated in the *Journal des Dames et des Modes*, 1912.

65.

66.

66. Small mother-of-pearl and jet buttons framed with a metal fillet, hailed as a novelty for masculine fashion in the 1910's. Collection *Palazzo Mocenigo*, Venezia. Photo Giacomelli.

67. Lathe for craft-manufacture of metal or fabric buttons used from early 19th century to the 1930's in all fully equipped haberdashery establishments. *I mestieri della moda a Venezia.*

conform with the mourning style then fashionable for women's clothes, jet buttons should be worn with the boiled shirt instead of pearl ones, which had become too common as the result of cheap imitations. These tails were designed by Kriegck, a famous London tailor who had opened a branch in Paris. The coat had a fairly high stick-up velvet collar and silk lapels. Five large round buttons led from the points of the jacket and closed it up to the chest. The waistcoat was in embroidered grey cashmere and the trousers narrow. The coat itself could be black, blue or grey, and was worn with a new type of opera hat that, instead of closing from top to bottom for holding under the arm, could be closed vertically like the three-cornered hat of old times.

Types of shirt-front button included platinum with a gold cross in the middle to imitate the sewing-thread of an ordinary button, and set with a *pavé* of tiny spangles of diamond-powder. The latter type was to be worn only for gala nights, and even then might be thought exaggerated, as the tradition of deliberate discretion for male elegance was by now firmly established.

Meanwhile matters had become complicated. In society circles one was "buttonholed" by those wishing to discuss the international situation. Prince Danilo waltzed at *Chez Maxime* with Anna Glavari, his Merry Widow, and the final splash of the *Belle Epoque* took place against the background-noise of sinister pistol-shots. For the first fifteen years of the century, the armies of the world, in the course of their various colonial wars, had transformed military uniforms by changing the former brilliant colours into something more sober and more in line with the need for camouflage, such as khaki for African campaigns, or the grey-blue of the Italian Army. Buttons also followed this trend. Instead of gilt metal with proud regimental emblems, as in the 18th century, and after experiments with bone, leather and other non-reflecting materials, the "strategic" button was made of undecorated metal and hidden beneath a flap.

However, metal buttons remained fully visible on the uniforms of senior officers and diplomats, who had other opportunities of showing off flashy buttons, on the occasion certainly less dangerous than in a trench at night.

The war that began in August 1914, after the assassination of the Austrian Crown Prince at Sarajevo, soon involved the whole of Europe.

Soldiers on all fronts were the involuntary "creators" of small objects, including aluminium or leather buttons, those most prized being ornamented with bits of stained glass from burnt-out cathedrals, the sad keepsakes of a sorrowful period.

68.

68. Celluloid or bone buttons, and hinged studs for fastening the starched collar to the neck-band.

69. Design for dress-uniform tunics for the Italian Army, with a metal button "the same for all ranks". *Le Uniformi Italiane secondo il codice Cenni.*

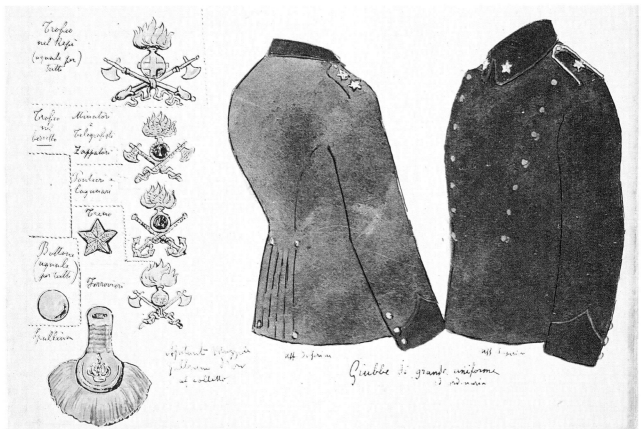

69.

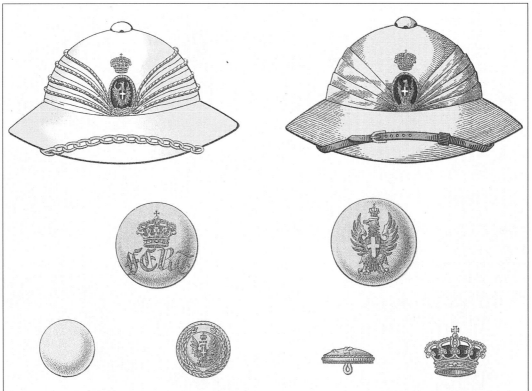

70. On the eve of the first world war uniform-buttons became "matt" and were hidden behind a pleat. *Le Uniformi Italiane* cit.

71. In the years immediately after the war, the *Raccolta Ufficiale delle Leggi e dei Decreti del Regno d'Italia* published the regulations for the uniforms of civilian State functionaries - diplomats, judges etc. Naturally this provided for metal buttons bearing the crest of House of Savoy.

TWENTY YEARS OF FASHION

72.

FEW BUT LOVELY

Immediately after the war, *Haute Couture*, which still spoke nothing but French and was to do so for many years to come, began to reorganize. Celebrated fashion-houses were joined by others, quickly patronized by the international clientele for whom Paris was the catalyzing pole of elegant eccentricity. In the early Twenties there was much talk of Worth, Doeuillet and Paquin; Poiret was less important now, but his place was being taken by his sister Nicole Groult. Lucien Lelong, Molyneux and Coco Chanel, with her very personal style, dominated the world fashion scene. A cosmopolitan, disenchanted and pushful society (which included *parvenues* from across the Atlantic anxious to become intellectual, refined and noble, thanks to marriages enabling them to add a coat of arms to their visiting-cards) thronged the salons of the "leaders of fashion", where each season brought a new cut, a new material or colour-scheme for dresses that were now definitely shorter and had fewer room

72. 1920's French metal and crystal button.

73. *Perlaine* suits, material by Rodier, a famous French clothier's, designed by Morgue for the *Gazette du Bon Ton*. 1922.

73.

for buttons. These are seldom mentioned and appear almost anonymously in the form of round leather buttons for raincoats, or metal ones for sports, travel or morning wear, like the barely convex ones of shiny steel that Paquin sewed onto a tailor-made and overcoat of "aubergine line" in blue gabardine (1922). They became showier in size and colour when, singly or in pairs and made of corozo, mother-of-pearl or crystal, they decorated soft flowing overcoats with shawl-collars. Dresses were cut slantingly, and were enveloping and flowing with drapery. The hook-and-eye were nearly always hidden, and often covered with thread of the same colour as the material. Press-studs, which had just reached the market, were great favourites, as they were discreet in size and easily done up. If the writer's memory is correct, these were known in her family as *"bottoncini tac"*, an onomatopoeia for the quick way they fastened.

Although as early as 1903 it had been possible to sublimate casein - the coagulant contained in milk - it was not used for buttons until after the First World War. The *Internationale Galalith Gesellschaft* of Hamburg specialized in producing plates and bars of casein formaldehyde, used for round or hemispherical buttons that could be turned or hotpressed on account of the malleability of this material in its paste stage, when it could also be coloured in the most varied shades.

The compactness and lightness of galalite buttons made it possible to engrave and paint them in fast colours.

Recently discovered and almost perfect plastics quickly replaced buttons of already rare tortoise-shell and horn. By 1923, mother-of-pearl could be imitated by adding metal filings to the paste, and new buttons in a wealth of colours never before seen were sewn on dresses in serried rows, almost always obliquely. After 1922 party-coloured buttons were fashionable: black and white, white and blue, brown and beige and red and blue.

74. *Promenade à Montmartre* is the name of this Bur outfit designed by Martin, with buttons all the way from the collar to the hem-line *La Gazette du Bon Ton, 1920*.

74.

52

As synthetic compositions are highly ductile and can be made in many shapes, unusual geometric designs were applied to round buttons as if to contest the perfect form of the circle, and three-dimensional geometric volumes appeared, such as cubes and bases of pyramids, with rounded angles in keeping with the flowing and tapered line of the *silhouette*.

53

75. Corozo and galalite buttons of the shape, colour and colour-combinations fashionable during the 20's, when dyes and plastics came into their own.

75.

54

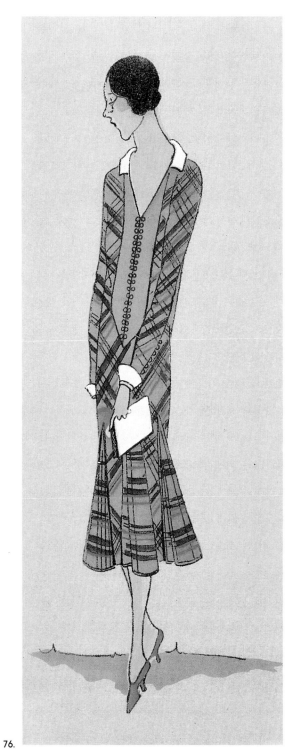

76.

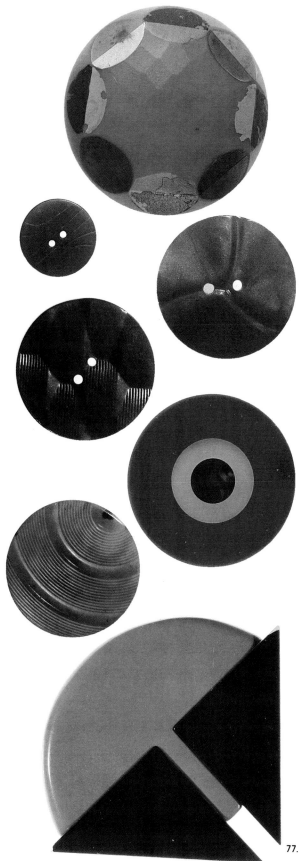

76. A dress of shot Scotch taffeta has a front closely fastened with two rows of little glass paste buttons. *Très Parisien*, 1925.

77. The top button, typical of early 20's trimming, is made of hand-decorated glass paste. The others and the belt-buckle are in celluloid and casein-formaldehyde.

77.

These little buttons were usually made of glass, and were borrowed from children's clothing. They mainly came from Austria and Bohemia, where production had been concentrated by the end of the 19th century, and also from Italy, where Ercole Moretti, after the middle of that century, had adapted the traditional Venetian glass-making industry by producing flat, domed and ball-shaped buttons of variously decorated glass that were much appreciated, exported and used in the Twenties.

78.

By 1925, buttons reappeared as ornaments rather than merely useful adjuncts. Worth, taking as model the women's dresses of the Mantuan court, designed a straight collarless *robe-manteau* with twenty-two gilt metal buttons running from the neck to the hem in parallel lines. Fashion called for decorative asymetrical fastenings by means of buttons on skirts, jackets, boleros and dresses. In the March number of the review *Fémina* for that year, the fashion-editress stated: "Putting to shame the *adorable simplicité* of previous seasons, this year's French collections show many surprising and complicated schemes of decoration. An orgy of little buttons outline each seam, are arranged in lace like patterns and weigh down the sleeves". Martine Rénier continues: "Were I a *couturier*, I should become obsessed; I'd wake up suddenly in the night in a cold sweat, after nightmares of being submerged and suffocated in an ocean of red, yellow, green and blue buttons".

79.

78. Glass and glass paste buttons, traditionally manufactured in Bohemia, Germany and England were much sought after in the 20's.

79. Glass paste buttons have metal or gem-stone inserts.

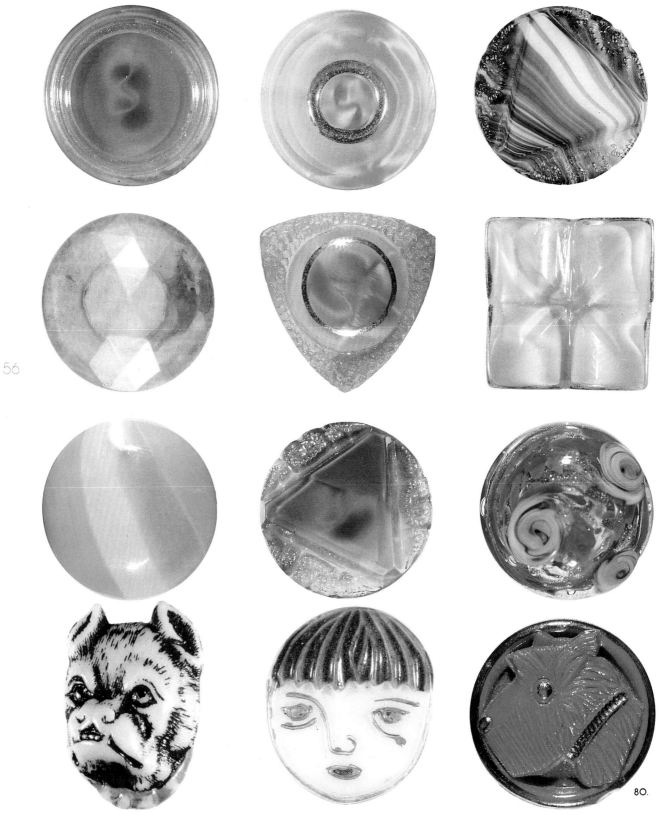

56

80.

80. An extraordinary selection of glass and glass paste buttons made in Venice, and typical of the 20's.

THE CHARM OF PARIS

1925 was a complex year, which imposed the geometrical forms proclaimed by the *Salon des Arts Décoratifs et Industriels Modernes,* held in Paris the *art déco* style. This stupendous exhibition demonstrated the possible applications of decorative arts to industrial products. The main aim was to persuade Frenchmen to buy French, but the idea of conciliating men and machines, which had perhaps previously been at odds, like the engineer and the architect or the artist and the craftsman, in order to harmonize beauty, efficiency and economic necessity, had succeded beyond all expectation. Whereas twenty-one fashion designers had exhibited at the *Exposition Universelle* held in 1900, there were seventy-two of them at the *Salon Déco*: fashion had obtained artistic recognition.

From across the Atlantic came the strains of Armstrong's jazz, and the Bauhaus was imposing a taste for sober functionality.

The fashionable woman wore a page-boy haircut, had a long-limbed *silhouette*, smoked, drank, drove a car, danced the Charleston and always looked to Paris as a guide to elegance. As Scott Fitzgerald wrote at the time: "Part of the magic of Paris lies on the fact that everything that happens there seems to have a connection with art."

81. Enamel buttons for a get-up designed by Bolin for *Vogue,* February 1931. W.Parker *I grandi disegnatori di Vogue.*

82. Set of enamel buttons with matching belt-buckle. The "Scotch" design hacks back to Art Nouveau motifs. *Donazione Vittoria Cohen,* Palazzo Mocenigo, Venice.

81.

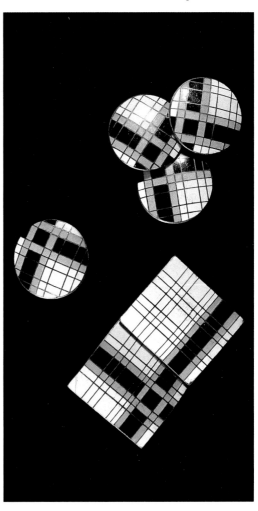

82.

The *art déco* philosophy also affected buttons, which followed its clean lines and regular precision. Dress-designers, and especially Coco Chanel, the woman dress-designer by definition, who came to the fore thanks to her sober elegance, her unprejudiced way of living and the famous names of her clients, began to think in terms of buttons, designing them for their personal, exclusive use. High-fashion buttons were manufactured by skilled but unknown craftsmen, who took the raw material - in the mid - Twenties almost always galalite sheets or bars - and turned them on a lathe or put them in moulds for heating in their workshop ovens. Often these same craftsmen made the costume - jewellery for *Mademoiselle* that was all the rage after the mid-Twenties.

Black and white were the signpost - colours of *art déco*, which favoured white metals (steel, silver or platinum for the rich). Buttons, too, were enamelled black, with a red stripe, on silver bases, and enamel buttons of regular geometrical shapes (hexagons, rhomboids and ovals) could be seen side by side with round, four -holed, mother-of-pearl ones. They appeared in rows on sweaters and

83.

58

84.

85.

86.

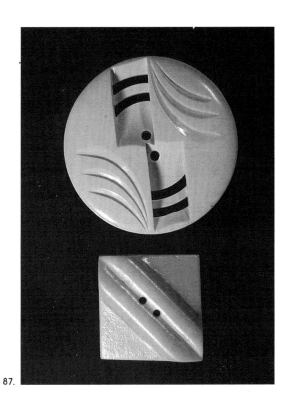

87.

cardigans, and, as cuff-links, closed the sleeves of the shirts Coco Chanel recommended during her "English period" (1925 - 1931), when she introduced into her collections of women's clothes a style based on the sporting elegance of the English gentry, with special reference to the Duke of Westminster, *Mademoiselle* Coco's official escort.

89.

88.

83. Black enamel buttons on white metal reflect the decorative motifs of the time in their design and strict colouring. 1925-30.

84.85. Bakelite button: red is the alternative colour to black and white. The triangular button of glass paste with metal trimming is typical of the prevailing taste.

86. The Art Déco button *par exellence*, with mother-of-pear and galalite strips.

87.88. White and coloured galalite in shapes and with inserts in line with Art Déco geometry. 1925-30.

89. Chanel. *Fémina* 1927.

MUCH DEPENDS
ON THE BUTTONS

Although men's fashion did not have the authoritarian weight or degree of fantasy of women's, it was evolving subtly and implacably, with variations of detail that imperceptibly changed its lines in the course of time. Thus an authoritative fashion-paper warned ladies to keep an eye on their husband's clothes, expecially regarding details which, in the course of a single season, could become out of date. Just as one would not go out with a missing waistcoat-button, said the writer, one must see to it that the jacket for afternoon wear did not pinch the waist, for the Twenties line called for softer jackets, tapering at the hips. The jacket still bore three buttons - of corozo, naturally - on which only one was done up. The middle button thus became the sign of a commitment to style, and its correct positioning the hall - mark of a good tailor, like the trouser buttons and those on the inside jacket pocket, engraved round the rim with the tailor's name.

60

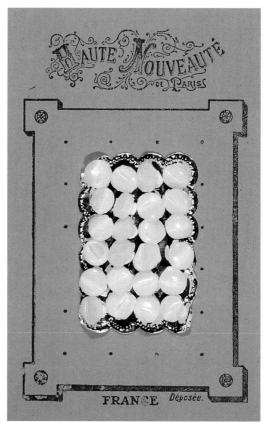

91.

90.

Although imitation mother-of-pearl was very popular, imitating very faithfully the natural product in its various shades, the latter resisted in the shape of the six little buttons, sewn in dozens on cardboard covered in silver paper, for the white evening waistcoat which was still, in the Twenties, the aristocratic garment for evening wear; and there was not a reception, dance, opera-performance, not a dining or drawing-room in which, after eight at night, the men were not turned out in evening dress.

90. Metal or galalite buttons bearing the tailor's name. These were sewn inside trousers to fasten braces, and on the inside pockets of the jacket.

91. A card of 24 mother-of-pearl buttons for men's shirts.

As for expensive buttons, beside pearls for evening dress, there were the cuff - links, to be found in the gentleman's jewel - case, and which will be dealt with later. But there were links less expensive, but just as necessary for true elegance.

The technique of incising crystal developed in England during the Sixties of the 19th century consisted in hollowing out the inside of a cabochon crystal to form a motif that was so painted as to appear three-dimensional. As subjects, cats, terriers and all animals connected with sport were very popular on cuff-links and waistcoat-buttons, and often on matching tie-pins. The mania for sporting, riding, hunting and yachting subjects was not confined to intaglios or to England, but, thanks to enamelling techniques, spread to the presents men received from their women-friends or wives, and helped to fill up those jewel-cases, especially in the Twenties when sport, movement, speed and dynamism became the order of the day for the modern man.

So here we have buttons again, always and everywhere. One brave soul started to count them, and concluded that, towards the end of the decade, a well - dressed man complete with overcoat might have on him no fewer than forty buttons, distributed among bone ones for his drawers, mother-of-pearl ones for his shirt, corozo and metal ones for his jacket, trousers, waistcoat and overcoat, not to mention leather buttons for sports clothes and rainwear and cord ones for his tails.

61

92. In England, the first blazers came out in the mid-29's and bore metal buttons.

MADAME SCHIAP

The dramatic Wall Street crash of October 1929 threw the financial world into chaos, and during the first years of the new decade a calmer style was unavoidable. Fashion followed this call to order: skirts grew longer, and the general line abandoned outrage and aggressiveness in favour of sloping flounces.

Despite these difficulties, Chanel continued to make models in her timeless style, adorning them whith fancy and goldsmith's buttons, thus combining inimitable elegance with common sense. In these years, embroidered and filigree buttons took their place beside traditional four - holed styles.

Elegant circles in Paris in the early Thirties were always talking about Elsa Schiaparelli, a dressmaker who had arrived in fashion circles thanks to the encouragement of the great Poiret, who had admired the elegance of an evening dress she had run up at home, cutting it out on the dining table without any knowledge of tailoring. She was driven by need (in the sense that it was a spur to ingenuity), worldliness (she knew members of the rich Anglo-Franco-American nomadic set and also famous artists) and a tenacity worthy of the greatest respect. Her talents favoured long clinging dresses of silk or canvas, with gold or silver borders that emphasized the originality and value of her creations. The artists among whom she loved to move involved her in the surrealist movement that exploded in the Thirties, and they designed for her wonderful motifs for embroidering on dresses and evening capes. Jean Cocteau's urn, made from two ambiguous profiles of gold thread, held a bunch of roses carried out in relief by

62

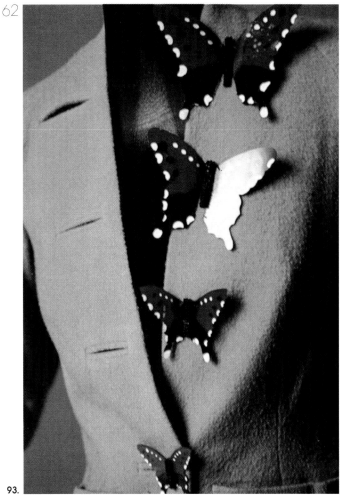

93.

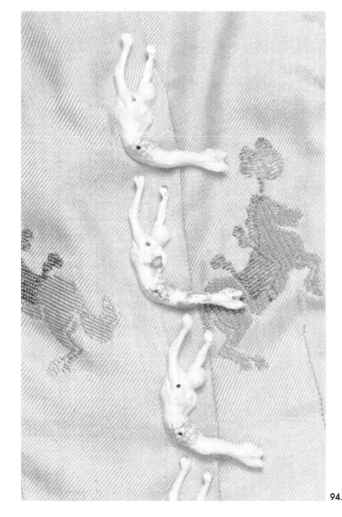

94.

Lesage, the Haute Couture embroiderer. Elsa Schiaparelli furnished her shop in the Place Vendôme with a divan in the shape of a mouth (lips being the most voluptuous symbol of Surrealism) designed by Salvador Dalì, and it was from his *City of Drawers* - an anthropomorphic cabinet - that she drew inspiration for a business - suit with two vertical series of real or false pockets representing drawers, with buttons representing handles. In addition, she used to dress Dalì's beautiful wife Gala free of charge, either out of admiration or friendship.

Buttons always intrigued Elsa Schiaparelli, who hated ordinary ones, which she would persecute with a reformer's zeal. It is said that she never bought one, even. Though such

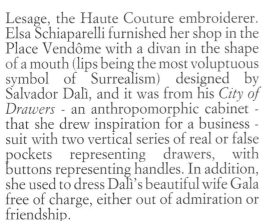

95.

93.94. The most extraordinary buttons used in *Haute Couture* during the 30's were disegned by Elsa Schiaparelli. Galalite butterflies and china acrobats for fancy jackets. W. Palmer, *Elsa Schiaparelli.*

95. A panorama of celluloid buttons from *Madame Schiap*, in the form of little boxes holding stamps, coffee beans, rice or oats. France late 30's.

REPUBLIQUE FRANÇAIS
2 F POSTES 2F

96.

absoluteness (which was a definite part of her character) may seem excessive, it is none the less true that as soon as *Madame* began her fashion career she began to invent and design exclusive, extravagant buttons.

She found an exceptional collaborator in the person of Jean Clément, who was not only a graduate of the *Ecole des Beaux Arts* but also the holder of a chemistry

degree. This background provided him with experience in dealing with colours and the plastics he cooked up in an electric oven. Palmer White, Schiaparelli's biographer, says that Clément was the

96. Special buttons for the lady in the Schiaparelli costume and gilt metal ones for the "cop" giving her street-directions. *Le Jardin des Modes,* 1936.

most brilliant accessory-designer Paris ever had. He worked exclusively for *Madame Schiap* who profited by his particular talents to get him to produce buttons of every shape and form, the colours of which were heightened up by means of a phosphorus paint.

Schiaparelli's buttons were chosen with devoted and surrealistic care, and placed wherever there was an opportunity and a space, even indeed on hats. They were often of enamel on a sculpted wooden, aluminium or other metal base, but there were others made of celluloid, china, amber, coloured glass, white jade, sealing-wax and the plastics galalite and bakelite.

For some of these wooden buttons, Clément used poker - work, a technique employed in Central Europe for wooden boxes. *Schiap* was the first to use china lemons, oranges, grapefruit and aubergines on tailor-mades and overcoats. Elsa and Jean must have had as much fun in designing them, having them made and placing them on garments as the clients had in wearing them, or perhaps even more, as the whim for new buttons was apparently inexhaustible, and during the Thirties at *Madame S'* s shop in the Place Vendôme one could find buttons in the shape of shoe-laces, crystal paper-clips holding flowers, spoons, ballerinas, ponies and lollipops. And then there were Christmas-tree bells, cork fishnet-floats, staples, gold metal dollar-signs, coffee-beans and sweet smelling cinnamon-berries. One day, apparently, they thought of magnets holding metal bars, but had to drop the idea as they were too heavy.

The search for perfection and accuracy of manufacture was such that Schiaparelli's leather buttons, sewn into all her sports clothes, had to be made by a saddler, so that the stitching be hand-made with two needles, as in the case of saddles. But one day *Madame* had the idea of mixing leather with fine cloth, and the saddler used his two needles to stitch crocodile-leather frogs and buttons into a black wool afternoon frock.

65

97.

97. Schiaparelli evening model with showy buttons.

66

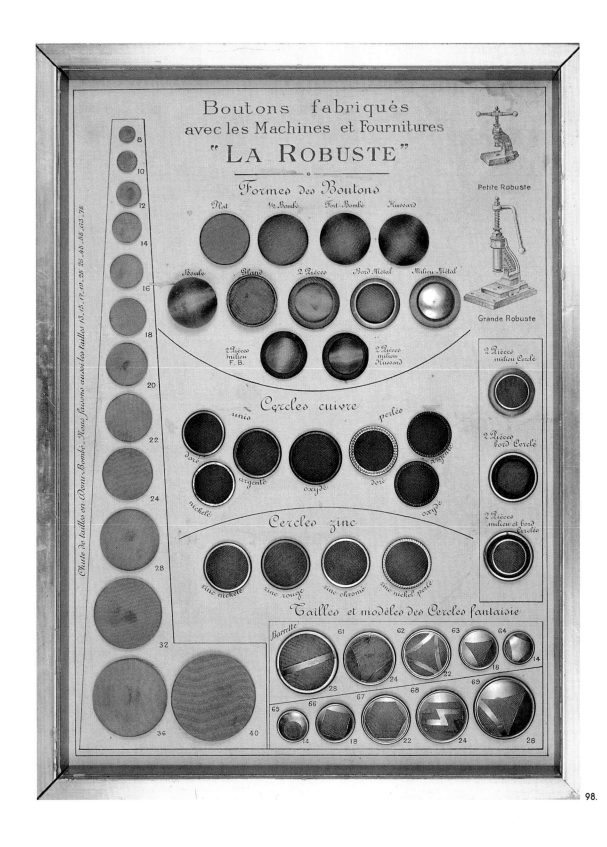

98. A small sample, for haberdashers' shops, of fabric and metal buttons made on *La Robuste* press. France 30's and 40's.

FANTASY FOR BUTTONS

The artistic revaluation of buttons spread out from the capital of fashion and reached Italy too in the Thirties. Despite the nationalistic efforts of the Fascist regime, the country was completely dependent on France in this respect. But the Italians had become very well organized for some time in button-manufacturing, and had wrested leadership in the market from Germany.

100.

99. Expensive glass paste, painted bakelite, "sculpted" metal and litography used in the late 30's for elegant dinner and theatre dresses. England. M. Tosa, *Vestiti da sera 1900...1940.*

100. American and German "jewel" buttons made of Heliotis mosaic or semi-precious stones for elegant women.

67

99.

Factories were traditionally concentrated in the province of Bergamo, where the manufacture of corozo buttons had begun at Palazzolo sull'Oglio in 1876. Nearby there were other factories specializing in the nails and bones of cattle, buffalo and deer horn, and mother-of-pearl. The Piacenza area was also the site of a flourishing industry, and a certain Dr. Vincenzo Rovera had made the first attempts there at producing corozo buttons with the help of a few workmen. The Italian industries that started up immediately after the war were artisans's cooperatives seeking better markets for their products, as may be seen from the statutes of several of them, the Bomisa for example, among whose members was one

of the first firms to introduce the integrated production - cycle. Also, at a time when men were all - powerful and unemployment rife, it is interesting to note that button factories were staffed by women, though this was due to the fact that the operation of balances and little presses was looked upon as light work,

101.102. "Figurative" buttons in hand-turned casein made by Italian craftsmen, and lacquered wooden buttons (skiiers and little flags) made in England. Late 30's, early 40's.

103.104. Fashion-magazines present smart accessories, including buttons, which can be made of leather or galalite with fake stitching. *Le Jardin des Modes,*. 1936.

suitable for feminine precision and delicacy of touch. The main raw material was "fruit", that is to say corozo, especially after it had been found that the nuts of the "dum" palm, growing in Eritrea and the Sudan, had the same properties as South American vegetable ivory, and were more accessible, Eritrea being still an Italian colony at the time.

As far as diameter was concerned, button measurements were universally established according to British "lines" (one line was equal to 0.635 mm.). Thickness was measured in millimetres and buttons were classified according to their intended use: for cloaks, uniforms, jackets, trousers, shirts, ladies suits, dresses, blouses, underwear, and for their

69

103.   104.

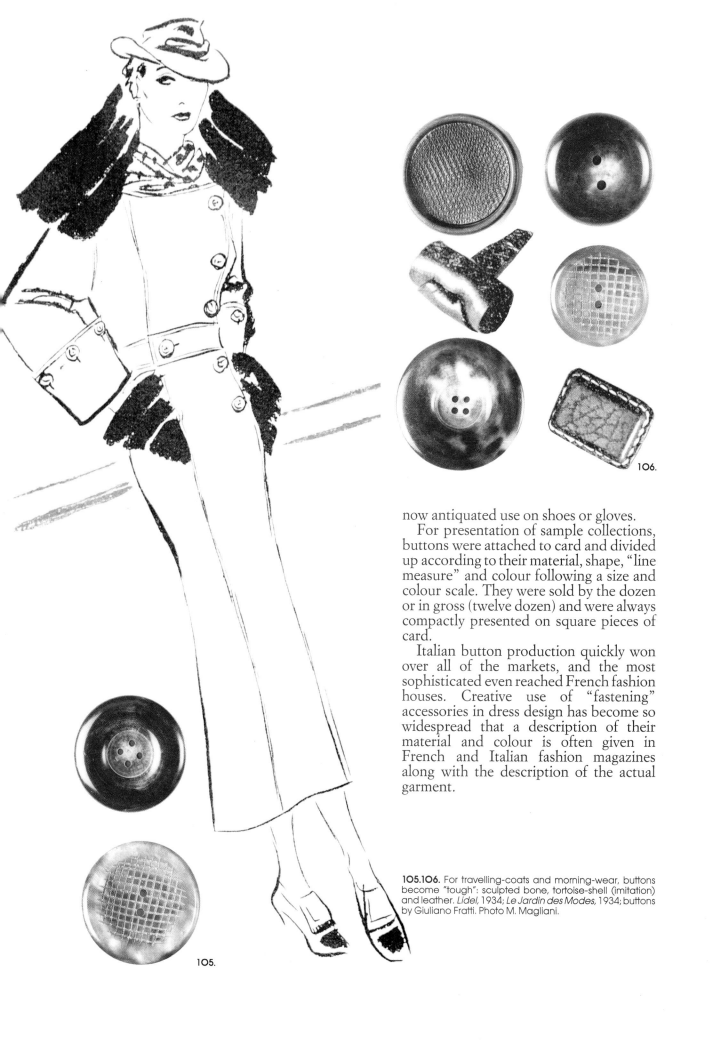

now antiquated use on shoes or gloves.

For presentation of sample collections, buttons were attached to card and divided up according to their material, shape, "line measure" and colour following a size and colour scale. They were sold by the dozen or in gross (twelve dozen) and were always compactly presented on square pieces of card.

Italian button production quickly won over all of the markets, and the most sophisticated even reached French fashion houses. Creative use of "fastening" accessories in dress design has become so widespread that a description of their material and colour is often given in French and Italian fashion magazines along with the description of the actual garment.

105.106. For travelling-coats and morning-wear, buttons become "tough": sculpted bone, tortoise-shell (imitation) and leather. *Lidel,* 1934; *Le Jardin des Modes,* 1934; buttons by Giuliano Fratti. Photo M. Magliani.

106.

105.

107.

BUSETTA AND BOTON

With buttons back in the forefront - no longer just the apple of the collector's eye, but brought to the speculative attention of fashion designers - it was inevitable that a diligent and specialized craft-type industry offering highly refined products would spring up beyond the bounds of mass production, and this development was to be welcomed and exploited by all those who had dedicated their creative talents and taste to fashion. This was in fact what happened in Milan at the end of the thirties when "Mister Button" - as he came to be known by his international clientele - set up shop in via Montenapoleone, which even then was the most chic street of the city. Giuliano Fratti set up a tiny *atelier*, adjacent workshop with about ten craftsmen, a lathe, scales and a machine for covering buttons with fabric in order to design and make exclusive buttons, and immediately all of

107. A dress of blue crease-resisting cloth with an unusual arrangement of white buttons. *Bellezza*, April 1944.

Milan's stylists, great and small, started to buy their buttons from him.

"Oh, what a lovely button ! I wish I knew where to put it !" exclaimed Ferrario, the dress-designer, when confronted with a large, shiny, showy corozo button. But he telephoned the next day to tell Fratti, the maker, that he had found exactly the place for this marvellous button -on a most elegant black tailor-made. So at least, for once it could be said that the button made the coat.

In the early Forties, Fratti's workshop was a magnet for everyone concerned with fashion, at the time when even the greatest optimists were doubtful about the future. The war had closed down one firm after another, and there were very few makers of high-fashion accessories left. They were strictly limited to local raw material: wood in its natural colour, or painted, varnished and poker-worked, in every shape and size, side by side with painted china buttons in the brightest colours and most varied designs.

By 1941, Fratti's buttons were being made of other autarkic, alternative, "wartime" materials, such as cork, straw and corn-cobs, and were photographed in the review *Bellezza*, a publication sponsored by the National Fashion Authority in replacement of the French and American periodicals unobtainable in wartime, in order to promote the image of a "victorious and seductive" Italy and to keep up the spirits of the womenfolk, who began to have other things to worry about.

108. "Ersatz" buttons are made of alternative materials such as wood, cork and corn-cobs. F. Jacassi collection.

108.

The art of "making do" also affected French creators, and "ersatz" products displayed the wildest fantasies. François Hugo, descendant of the poet, designed a series of fancy buttons for Worth, Hermès and Schiaparelli in electric cable.

Even at the darkest hour, clothes had to be fastened, especially in cold weather. Haberdashery shops were out of zip-fasteners, unobtainable because made of metal. The national emergency decreed by the Fascists requisitioned iron, copper, brass even, and small metal objects had practically disappeared, so that people began to transfer buttons from one piece of clothing to another, trying to combine colour, size and suitability with proper regard to the Goddess of elegance presiding, despite everything 'over ladies' costumes.

109. Military uniforms are always full of metal buttons, and Fascist uniforms bore showy ones, with the "fasces" well in view. The most enthusiastic Fascists also wore enamelled cuff-links bearing the emblem. U.Pericoli, *Le divise del Duce.*

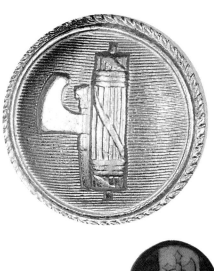

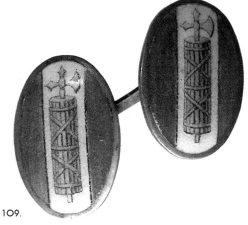

109.

74

110.

111.

110. Craftsmen's buttons of casein and rhodoid (a transparent composition), with metal inserts. Italy, 40's.

111. "Snakeskin" on casein, made of casein and of painted china. These were the most sought-after Italian buttons in the 40's.

112. A super buttoned jackets, in vogue during the early 50's. *Marie Claire,* 10 December 1949.

113.

Ornamental concern was shifted to buttonholes, which had always been the close companion of buttons, so much so that a popular Venetian expression for "as thick as thieves" might be read as "like the button and its hole".

The hole -the buttonhole- is "the eye-shaped slit cut into the edge of part of a garment, that is sewn and reinforced with buttonhole-stitch so that the button sewn on the corresponding part of the garment can enter it, thus keeping the garment

113. Tunic evening-dress probably by Elsa Schiaparelli, fastened behind with a series of jewel-buttons. Eric's drawing appeared in *Vogue America* in 1946. W. Parker, *op. cit.*

114. Transparent ground-glass, gold-decorated china, a metal and blue strass dragon-fly and a enamel decoration on plexiglass are specimens of jewel-button for very fashionable dresses of the second half or the 40's.

114.

itself closed or buttoned", according to the *Vocabolario della Crusca*, which refers to illustrious earlier examples such as the *Riformagioni del Comune di Firenze* of 1355 and '56, when attempts were made to moderate the exorbitant luxury of ornamental buttons. The decree ran :" No button may be worn on any garment which has no buttonholes to receive such buttons". And when in addition the buttonholes were made of precious metal, like the silver gilt ones ordered by Duke Galeazzo Maria Sforza from his tailor Panigarola in 1475, it only made matters worse.

At a moment of decorative exuberance in the 1910's, women's buttonholes were "encircled" with silk cord, trimming, plaid taffetas and on woollen garments, contrasting and often highly-coloured satin. When cut on the slant and visibly bigger than the corresponding buttons, in the Thirties, and in the best tailoring tradition, the buttonhole-stitch was completed on the outside with silk or shiny cotton thread.

Very sporting clothes had buttonholes of the same material, or leather, and "family" encyclopaedias of the time explained how to make these, repair them if they became unsewn and mend them almost invisibly, especially when they were part of clothes to be "turned", an operation much in vogue at times of great shortage and hardship.

Proper tailor's buttonholes are hand sewn in buttonhole-stitch. An article in *Fili Moda* for June 1943 explained how the buttonhole is cut straight: the two edges are then sewn together. The *Vergolina*, a cord sold in different widths, which guarantees non deformation, solidity and maximum resistance, is then inserted.

Wartime clothes for elegant occasions did not lose sight of the practical need for warmth, and often were made of wool, wool mixture or substitutes with a vague similarity of name (*Lanital*, a fibre made from milk). Jackets often bore frogging, which not only guaranteed good fastening but had a decorative function. Buttons could be made of material, usually shiny black like the former "brandenburgs", or Arabian *al hamir* of clover-shaped silk cord with the tape button typical of the nomads' burnous.

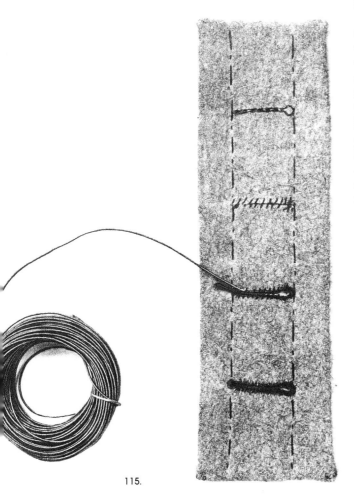

115.

115. Sewing-lesson for perfect buttonholes using *Vergolina*. *Fili Moda*, 1943.

A FLOWER IN THE BUTTONHOLE

"A flower that has passed from a lady's *corsage* to the buttonhole of a young knight's tunic, that's gallantry", according to Lorenzo Magalotti, an eighteenth century man of letters, who continues " but God help us if it ends up in the buttonhole of a State Councillor or a Magistrate!"

Two centuries later, in the 1990's, a flower in a buttonhole is a sign of elegance and gallantry that has assumed different concrete and symbolic meanings, and also a symbol and declaration of pride in a task accomplished.

In which buttonhole ? In that of the left lapel of man's jackets and overcoats, in

116.

memory of the expensive buttons on the tail-coats of the early 19th century. In the case of evening dress, where the languid gardenia or (nowadays) politically-coloured red carnation are the preferred flowers, a little loop is sewn behind the lapel to held the stem, a tailor's refinement for the man of the world.

The same buttonhole can harbour a series of more or less rigid-stemmed flat buttons, most often of coloured enamel, but also in repoussé or stamped metal, which men have adopted since the end of the First World War as a reassuring sign of their belonging to some association or other. Buttonhole-badges or coloured ribbons show political partisanship, or membership of knighthood orders, professional association and so on, down to the "sports clubs" which, in Italy, are by definition those of football-supporters. The writer remembers the notorious "bed-bug", a tricolour shield traversed by the Fascist emblem, which all males from the age of fourteen to the tomb used to wear during the twenty years that regime lasted. After the last war, the buttonhole became the scene of an outburst of symbols and badges, a glance of which was enough to show an observer what were the "passions" of his vis-à-vis.

In South America, where football is even more popular than in Italy -were that possible- the famous trainer Helenio Herrera reports that badges are made of gold and precious stones, on a scale suitable for those who believe that size is a sign of wealth. As some supporters are not content with this, they add a diamond for every championship won by their team, so that, meeting an *aficionado* on a sunny day, one runs the risk of being blinded by his brilliants.

But that is not the whole story of badges, because they have spread to the lapels of unisex jackets, where they advertise the various trends of the time. Ducks and foxhounds, geometrical designs in enamel, gilt or white metal, alternate with nautical and sports motifs, and Far West symbols, with the speed required by those who wish always to be up to the minute, even in the slightest details.

117.

116. Bespoken tailoring calls for accurate finish in the choice of buttons and the perfection of the buttonhole and "its" flower. *La Moda Maschile*, May-June 1951.

117. "National" football-team badges of precious stones belonging to Helenio Herrera and metal and enamel buttonhole-badges. Bomisa, 80's.

118.

118. A perfect buttonhole painted by Gnoli. L.Carluccio, *Domenico Gnoli.*

THE REFLOWERING OF FASHION
THE FIFTIES AND THE SIXTIES

119. A Schiaparelli dress with original enamel buttons. *Harper's Bazaar,* 1950.

119.

82

MISTER BUTTON'S CONFESSIONS   121.

Ever since the birth of fashion, the best way of getting over bad temper and mishaps has been to go and buy a new dress, or at least so the ladies of *café society* believed in the Forties. So it is easy to imagine what happened immediately after the Second World War, and the zeal for renewal with which fashion-designers set to work again.

The Dior phenomenon seized hold of Paris, and by the end of the Forties French *Haute Couture* dominated the world, as it had before the war. Italy followed suit with *modellisti* who paid to attend the Paris dress-shows and bought either original models, patterns for them or the right to copy them for sale to Italian dressmakers. The purchase of a single model with the right to copy it meant that the buyer had acquired all necessary information about the fabric and accessories, including buttons and decorations. Giuliano Fratti joined the

120. Outfit with summer jacket in printed cotton, early 50's. Showy buttons that can also be of straw and casein, in the shape of little bows, and casein-and-pristal.

121. Fine Italian buttons, early 50's: pristal and casein, hand decorated china, mother-of-pearl and casein.

120.

model-buyers, and bought original buttons and *bijoux*, and the right to copy them, from the French houses. "So that when the skilful Italian dressmakers came to the model - houses in Milan after the Paris shows in order to update their collections, they could also buy original buttons and reproductions in perfect imitation of the most famous high fashion of the day". When, in the early Fifties, the "made in Italy" style began to attract the attention and interest of the world's fashion press and of customers at the Florence shows, Giuliano's famous buttons became celebrated throughout the continent.

In its issue of 14 May 1949, *Marie Claire* speaks of the decorative function of buttons on a coat, and praises the button - creators who have "assumed the responsibility for inventing buttons of every shape, colour and quality".

"Our Lady of Fashion" seems to have had a great "appetite for buttons", which

122. Strass and glass beads, resin and metal, painted casein and galalite are the materials for fancy buttons in 50's fashion. Giuliano Fratti.

123. A selection of decorated galalite and casein buttons for the printed silk jacket. 50's.

124. *Robe-manteau* by Lanvin for Elizabeth Arden. Buttons of galalite, pristal and fabric, wood and glass, by Giuliano Fratti. *Marie Claire,* 14 May 1949.

125. Grey wool jacket with two panels buttoning in front and behind. Lattuada design. *Marie Claire,* 16 September 1950.

126.-129. Summer *Haute Couture* tailor-made presented in *L'Officiel* of April 1952 and three American models "buttoned" in galalite and metal. *Harper's Bazaar,* February 1952.

124.

125.

128.

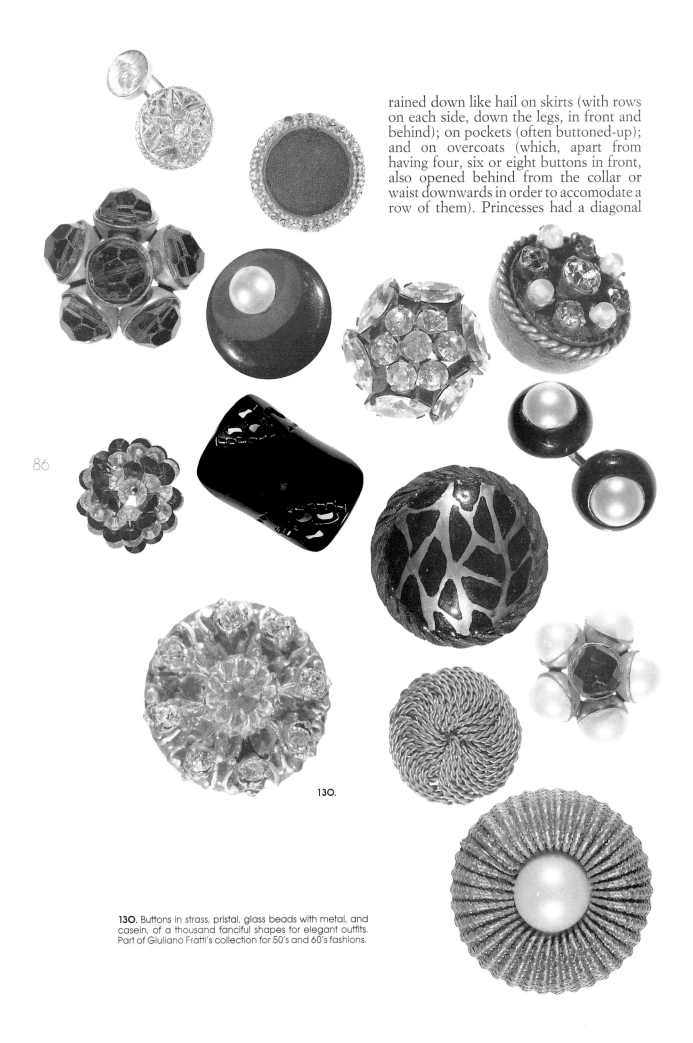

rained down like hail on skirts (with rows on each side, down the legs, in front and behind); on pockets (often buttoned-up); and on overcoats (which, apart from having four, six or eight buttons in front, also opened behind from the collar or waist downwards in order to accomodate a row of them). Princesses had a diagonal

130.

130. Buttons in strass, pristal, glass beads with metal, and casein, of a thousand fanciful shapes for elegant outfits. Part of Giuliano Fratti's collection for 50's and 60's fashions.

cross - over, and were always fitted to the figure with buttons, and there were extravagant buttonings, on the shoulders, along the sleeves and on the very low - cut evening dresses.

Tailor-mades, overcoats and *robes-manteaux* had classic horn, mother-of-pearl or galalite buttons, not forgetting fancy ones of wood, bamboo, leather and cork. Often the overcoat or three-quarter length coat, very fashionable at the time, was fastened at his high, soft collar with one huge showy button.

During the Fifties, buttons had to be of the same shade as the garment, and many little workshops for dressmakers' accessories set aside a corner for dyeing them according to samples. In fashion were four - holed galalite buttons, almost always manufactured industrially, concave and with a little raised rounded edge. These were known as *Molyneuxs* (it seems that the Anglo-French designer was the first to put them on his dresses), and a few extra buttons were always dyed and delivered with the dress, in case the wearer lost any.

87

131.

131. "Model" button in sculpted pristal with silvered surface. England, 50's.

132. Throughout the 50's and part of the 60's, elegant women wore, for smart little evening engagements, a dress on wool crepe, silk crepe or jersey, provided it was black. The dress was always pragmatically brightened up with a rope of pearl and often with jewel-buttons of strass.

132.

AN INDUSTRIAL FATE

Starting in the boom - years of the mid - Fifties, enlarged markets and a more widespread desire to be "dressed in the latest fashion" led, by the Sixties, to an ever - increasing clientele. Fashion was no longer exclusive, and the ready - made branch, which had always been the Cinderella of the industry, adjusted to the new requirements by organizing itself at a smarter level, thus giving rise to a new fashion which could exist with dignity side by side with the traditional "high class" one.

Ready - mades invaded all sectors of clothing - production, involving an increasing number of workers and calling for new types of work - organization. The buttons created by designers for high fashion were also caught up in the whirlwind, and had to adjust to an increased demand for functionality, originality and cost. Novelties in the line had quickly become more beautiful, brilliant, colourful and suitable for the industry's needs.

It was especially in this respect that catastrophes occurred at first. In the early Sixties industrial button-production could still not provide an adequate response to the needs of "fashion", even though the industrial product already consisted of "good buttons", which neither faded, darkened nor rusted. In addition, it was very important that buttons should be suitable, in their shape and the placing of their holes, for the button - sewing machines that had been in use for some time already in ready - made clothing factories.

Meanwhile, chemical synthesis was producing new materials for button-making. Urea-based resins had already replaced galalite in the Forties, and by the Fifties acrylic resins, which were worked like galalite, proved themselves excellent as regards brilliance and durability. The best known of these resins was plexiglass, the transparent component of various buttons, where it had replaced glass paste.

133. Industrial plexiglass buttons, made of a resistant glossy, transparent acrylic resin, machined in the 1950's as though they were galalite.

133.

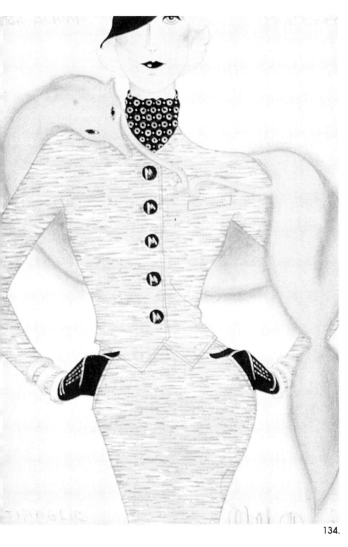

Often, for a more vivid effect, the resin embalmed pieces of fabric (of the dress) little coloured beads or bits of metal.

Polyestyrene and nylon buttons were also appearing, followed by acetates and polyester, both of which found favour with manufacturers; the former because of its chromatic qualities, the latter, which began slowly to replace it, on account of its low cost and ease of working, making for mass-production. Polyesters make it possible to obtain various chromatic effects by the use of additives such as "essence of pearls", which gives translucence.

However, the new techniques were not sufficient to solve all the problems, at least not before a balance had been found between the button industry and the ready-to-wear styles. This was brought about by producing seasonal samples presented in good time, and in line with the trends and colours required by the garment industry.

Ideas became cleaner and delays shorter when the new prophets of fashion - the ready-to-wear designers - turned their creative energies to the field of accessories and chose the samples offered personally instead of through representatives. In the next stage, they designed buttons themselves.

This inspiration was the result of the need to personalize each garment as far as possible, going beyond the mere name on the label. Though many designers who also produced fabrics stamped the selvedges of their cloth with their name repeated at regular intervals, others invented a stylized monogram for reproduction on their metal or plastic buttons, like the W A of Walter Albini or the K S of Ken Scott, who began the series of signed Italian buttons in the late Sixties and early Seventies.

134.

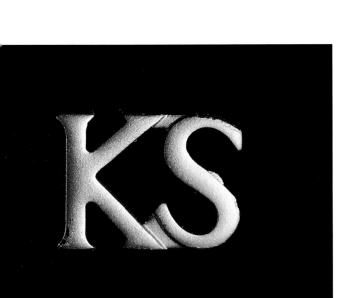

135.

134. Walter Albini designed for a *Vogue* publicity *groupage* a tailor-made that showed off the buttons. He was the first designer to put his W-for-Walter on his buttons, an example that was soon to be followed by other colleagues. *Walter Albini, Uno Stile nella Moda.*

135. A metal button with Ken Scott's logo produced by Bomisa.

136.

A METALLIC STORY

Metal buttons, the most noble ancestors of all the tribe, have been the "glittering" protagonists throughout human history, especially once they appeared, crested and mottoed, on military uniforms. Complicated events brought them from lowly to the highest position, from the mud of trenches to the altars of glory, the show-cases of museums, and to recycling, when, after the Second World War, they were sold with surcharged designs to hide their bellicose origins.

The arrogance of their martial air has fascinated whole generations of men, and seems destined to endure now that the metal button has moved from a strictly military use to other types of jacket, so

136. One phase of metal-button-making in the Bomisa factory.

that after army uniforms, college blazers and servants' liveries, crowned, monogrammed or otherwise decorated metal buttons now adorn the jackets of all the categories, communities, corporations, associations and so forth that use them as a means of identifying their profession.

But even a passing mode must have its hour of glory; at the end of the Fifties, when the blazer had invaded every single male wardrobe, these blue jackets were fastened with one or two rows of metal buttons echoed by small ones on the sleeves, and stamped with all kinds of motifs, principally coats of arms and shields, weapons and nautical devices. The upwardly mobile industrial "sea dogs" of the boom-years, with their flashy yachts and gladioli in the cockpit, fitted proudly into their new role, wearing blue jackets and buttons engraved with anchors.

On the feminine side, once Coco Chanel reopened her salon in 1954 after its wartime interruption, she went for gold metal buttons in her personal and ever-up-to-the-minute style as a type of costume jewellery. Her distinctive tailor-made had

137. Some examples of the classical and fancy "repertory" of Bomisa, which specialized from the 50's onward in metal and enamel buttons. Bomisa supplies metal buttons for many of the world's armies, and will fulfill orders for any subject, like the dachshund in white metal ordered by a customer as a present for his wife, who was particulary fond of her dog.

137.

91

buttons everywhere; at the waist, on pocket-flaps and sleeves; and her shirt-dresses too had buttons, with the famous lions' heads on a backing of material, leather or even mother-of-pearl, that also appeared on the inside hems of her coats and skirts. The old lady's passion for gilt metal went beyond mere buttons, and thousands of kilometres of cables and chains, which not only decorated collars and neck - openings, but provided handles for bags, encircled the hips and even found their way into the insides of tailor - mades, thus increasing for a long time the production of what, with the buttons, were known as metal sundries.

The manufacture of metal buttons (usually of brass for the best quality ones), whether "closed" buttons, made of two parts fitting together hermetically, or all in one piece, begins with cutting out of a round from a brass ribbon. This is then die

138.

139.

138.139. From the moment when Coco Chanel invented her inimitable style, her tailor-mades have called for millions of buttons bearing the metal Assyrian lion's head, in fabric, leather, mother-of-pearl and galalite, and as many again with her crossed "C"'s. Chanel buttons and chains were made under licence in Italy by Giuliano Fratti until 1972. *Annabella,* 3 March 1966.

- stamped, after which the two parts are assembled, the shank soldered on and the whole piece cleaned. It then goes to the "galvanic bath" from which it emerges in all its shining glory. A small but important secret, which makers only reveal reluctantly, is the core (chalk ? clay ? cardboard ? They used to use 5 lire coins, but they proved too expensive) that goes inside the closed button to give it weight, but not too much or, once sewn on, it will hang down. In this connection, Italian admirals' buttons sit close to the cloth and do not hang down because the back, where the shank is attached, is concave instead of convex. The specifications for military buttons are strictly binding as regards weight, size, thickness, milling and immersion-time in the galvanic bath, which for the Americans, who require buttons to be very shiny, lasts two minutes longer. The Carabinieri do not sew on their crested silver buttons with thread, but insert them directly into holes backed by a split-ring.

93

140.

140. A button with the Admiralty anchor from among Bomisa's samples.

141. Seafarer's blazer with classic metal buttons bearing marine motifs. *La Moda Maschile,* July-August 1958.

141.

142.

143.

144.

142.143.144. Three generations of military buttons made by Bomisa for the army at different times in the history of the Italian Armed Forces: Royal Navy buttons (until 1946), the Carabinieri flame and the "multiarm" button common to all corps. Silvered buttons are for the generals.

145. Armies of women in the world over were wearing straight tailor-mades in the 60's, fastened with nearly always convex buttons, made of galalite, "dyed by sample"

THE BUTTON WAR
OF THE SEVENTIES

146.

HIDDEN, ESPECIALLY

The student revolt that broke out in Paris in May 1968 and spread to the rest of Europe concluded drastically, and two years too early, an opulent, swaggering decade and also the post - war era, by confronting middle-class industrial society and the consumer civilization with their responsibilities.

In this climate of protest and reform, in which accusations were levelled more at intentions than facts, fashion withdrew to less ostentatious positions, and buttons, when not being used as ammunition for catapults, along with ball-bearings and lead packet-seals, were hidden behind the front flaps of parkas and anoraks, the preferred dress of young revolutionaries. Many were four - holed hemispherical or flat buttons, or large iron-coloured press-studs for fastening the blue jeans and denim jackets worn by the typical youth - swarms of the time. These buttons were always stamped with the brand - name of the maker then in vogue: Lee, Levi's or Wrangler.

146.147. The jeans era coined special buttons in "rude", antirust metal. Designer buttons for jeans were just beginning to appear. *Ferré Jeans, Valentino Jeans* by Bomisa; advertisement in *Uomo Vogue*.

147.

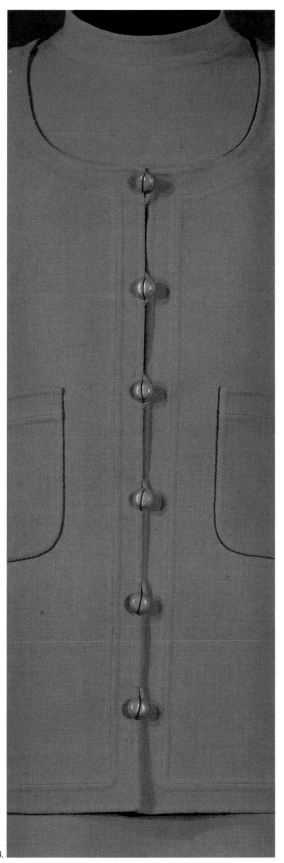

Consequently, in the Seventies buttons were an almost exclusively functional accessory, mainly used for sports - clothes. There was still some production of convex leather buttons, irreplaceable for Loden overcoats (unisex, green, lined and with a double - buttoning flap on the cuffs and a pleated split up the back), as well as real or artificial wood and horn buttons that went well with the "casual look", an expression defining comfortable, rational but stylistically commonplace clothing. The crisis did not affect buttons alone, but they paid more dearly than other items. The causes of this sudden eclipse are complex, but the considerable drop in demand was certainly due to excessive production-costs, combined with a rather radical change of fashion.

149.

148.149. Details of Giuliano Fratti's buttons for a Mila Schön's model of 1965. Industrial buttons of plastic with metal, peculiar to the 60's.

148.

During the first years of the Seventies, fashion tended towards a unisex levelling of styles, and as in these cases it is always the feminine side that adopts the clothes and attitudes normally reserved for men, trousers, jackets, wide shoulders and narrow hips gave rise to styles that left little space for fancy buttons, and resulted in an androgynous line. These clothes were

151.

150.

150. New products of chemical synthesis can provide perfect imitations of natural materials. Buttons made of urea resin, polyamids and nylon are exactly like their predecessors in wood and leather. Details from *Corozite,* 1987 samples.

151. Buttons "run after" by fashion must always have that little extra something. Giuliano Fratti, 60's.

152. Gild daisy-shaped buttons abound on Sorelle Fontana's narrow overcoat and on Ballin's red laquered shoes. *Domina,* August 1969.

153. Industrial buttons meet the needs of the ready-to-wear trade by using new synthetics, almost always decorated with metal.

98

153.

fastened with metal or other flat four -
holed discs, which could be of mother-of-
pearl or "dirty petrol, mother-of-pearl
style" in the words of Angelo Fenili, of the
third generation in his firm's button -
industry, who continues "but the effect is
so good that the button has to be subjected
to mechanical treatment before one can
realize that it isn't real mother - of - pearl".
It is hard to decide how far the two factors
above were interdependent; in any case,
they both formed part of a more general
unease.

154.

155.

154. The stylistic intemperance of the 70's invades women's *garde-robes* in the search for a "divertion" that has nothing to do with elegance. Buttons alone are saved. Model by Danielle, Elviretta buttons. Early 70's. Photo Ente Italiano della Moda.

155. The metal accessories for this giddy model for speed-boating (Eva Sabbatini 1972) are by Bomisa.

156.

157.

156. Neapolitan tailor Nativo doesn't want to be thought conservative and he places the buttons and fastenings on his jackets in an unusual way. *Nativo by San Giorgio.*

157. The last buttons called "La Ferramenta" made by Giuliano Fratti who ceased working in 1972, after being hailed as "Mister Button" by all the "High Priests" of international fashion.

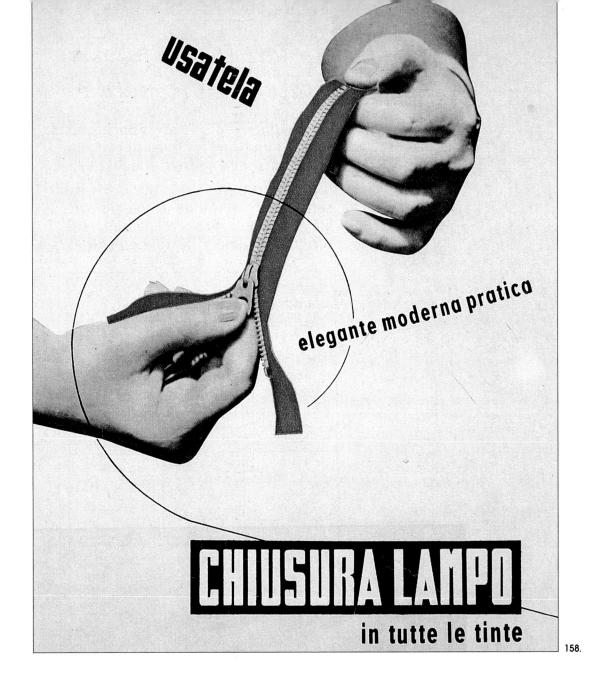

usatela

elegante moderna pratica

CHIUSURA LAMPO

in tutte le tinte

158.

PITILESS COMPETITION

Meanwhile, an aggressive and very dangerous attitude was growing up in Western Europe, which gave rise in Italy to what became known as the "leaden years", and the gloomy atmosphere of the time affected the philosophy of dress.

Extreme nonconformity led to ... uniform. Everyone was wearing blue jeans and denim jackets almost all the time. Paramilitary, bellicose and expensively poverty-stricken clothes (or disguises?), became the fashion. The fastening of hide, leather or battle-dress clothes, all in brownish shades, took the shape of leather thongs passed through eye - holes, or metal buckles and spring-clips of threatening appearance, as well as metal - toothed zip-fasteners of every dimension, ostentatiously worn on long or short jackets, overalls and tunics - all, of course, unisex.

The first "continuous automatic closure for clothing" was patented in the United States in 1851 by Elias Howe, much better-known for his contribution to the

158. Appropriate advertisement for the "Zip-Fastener". *Gemma*, 1939.

invention and distribution of the sewing-machine. However, the invention, consisting of "a series of hooks united by a small cord that runs up and down teeth" was never marketed. Only in 1894 did Messrs. Lewis Walker and Whicomb L. Judson organize the Universal Fastener Company for exploiting the latter's patent for an automatic fastening made of hooks and eyes opened and closed by means of a slide.

A patent was taken out in 1917 for a fastener with all the characteristics of the modern zip. Its inventor, Mr. Sundback, pointed out that the main requirement for making it workable was the elimination of the hooks. One of the first uses of the new invention was its application to the flying - jackets of the U S Navy; its first general civilian use was on the rubber galoshes made by the firm of Goodrich, which also patented the name of zipper, *chiusura lampo* in Italian, synonymous with the fastener: this became the brand-name of a firm specializing in this item during the Thirties; and the name has stuck.

Since its appearance, the zip-fastener has been one of the "utility" accessories, for working-trousers and overalls and women's coats and skirts, on the hips or the front, always behind a pleat to hide its unaestethetic appearance. By the mid-Sixties, the zip, with its toothy smile, seemed to have eaten up all the buttons.

Arrogant, irate and gnashing its teeth, it is everywhere, on jackets and coats, furs and children's clothes, wherever fastening is required. Buttons have disappeared, and their makers, at least those specializing in metal ones, had to counter-attack. They began by palming off the intruder a showy slide in the shape of a big ring or an engraved or enamelled metal plate, which made the zip more personal ... and less dangerous for the button-trade.

159.

159. Metal and enamel personalized zip-fastener slides. Bomisa.

160.

161.

162.

163.

164.

165.

160.161.162. Enamel portrait on bronze, Italy, late 18th century. Blue flowers enamelled on silver, France 19th century. Floral motifs enamelled on a metal base, England, mid-19th century. R. Goni Collection.

163.164. Pair of waistcoat buttons with enamelled figures on gilt metal. France ? last quarter of 18th century. Collezione Corinaldi-Bomisa.

165. Designer buttons. *Moon and Stars*, Kaffe Fassett, England c. 1960. *Tender Buttons* Collection.

THE MOST BEAUTIFUL BUTTON OF ALL

After a period of discomfort and perplexity, buttons succeeded in meeting the zip's challenge by concentrating on the highly-specialized sphere of sports clothes and garments requiring hermetic but not "constricting" fastenings.

The sponsors of this revaluation of the button were the ready-to-wear stylists, who discovered its personalizing and advertising value, apart from considerations of taste and fashion. The new trend began with monogrammed buttons, which true connoisseurs deem the most beautiful of all.

The most perfect enamelled buttons in the world come from the leader in this field, the firm of Bomisa, which has been producing them since 1945, when they began to use special enamels for military sleeve - and shirt - flashes.

166. Set of opaque enamel on metal buttons. The style of drawing suggests that of the early 1900's, but they are in fact "artistic buttons" made around the 30's. V. de Buzzaccarini Collection.

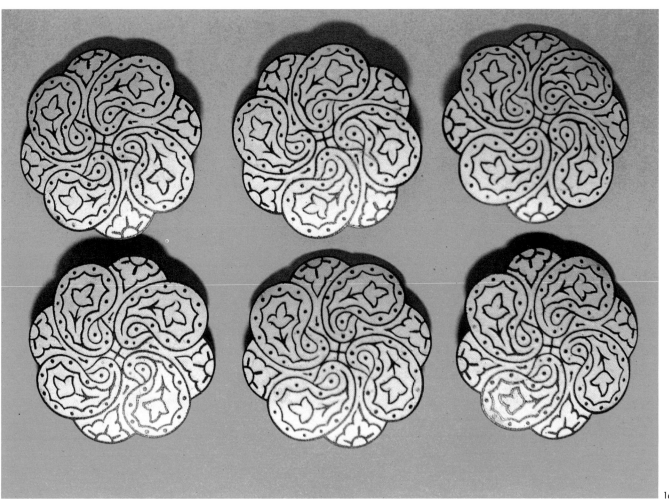

166.

167.

makes the metal parts brilliant. Bomisa states explicitly that their secret patent enamelling process is the best in existence.

The particular virtue of the enamel button lies in its colours, which can be as many as four or five. They are brilliant and distinct, forming the design, device or monogram on the face of the button, and can vary according to a chromatic scale embracing all possible combinations.

Designs can be submitted by the customer in the case of the best-known ready-to-wear and tailoring houses (or those which aspire to become so), and by companies, associations or clubs wishing to show their members' affiliation in this way.

167. Enamel on brass button, and its back. Craft work, 50's. V.de Buzzaccarini Collection.

168. Some examples of the vast number of enamel buttons made by Bomisa, the unanimously recognized specialist for this type of work.

The excellence of this work depends on the engraving, which must be perfect, and the treatment required to make the metal (usually brass) porous, so that it can absorb the enamel. This consisted, from 1956 onwards, of glass enamel heated in an oven to 1200 degrees, replaced after 1964 by synthetics. Both these types have replaced varnish paints, which can "rub off" with time.

The final operations are those of polishing and cleaning the enamel, and immersion in the "galvanic bath", which

168.

169.

170.

169. Personalized cuff-links and shirt or jacket buttons for the elegant men.

170. For the height of elegance, the dinner jacket should be worn with matching cuff-links and shirt buttons, better still if they are made of precious stones. *The Man at His Best.*

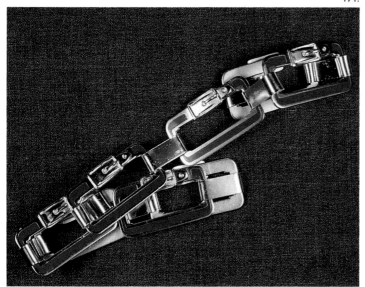

The series began in 1969 with Gucci, the world - famous Italian leather firm, and the Roman tailoring-house of Brioni, followed in 1970 by Ken Scott and in '72 by Roberta di Camerino, who also included enamelled belts in her collection. The list of clients for personalized buttons now includes everyone, from Valentino Garavani to Cardin, Dior, Krizia, Armani, Enrico Coveri, Laura Biagiotti, Yves Saint-Laurent and Franco Moschino, to name only the best-known. The brilliance and colour-combinations of the many enamel buttons used in international collections have often replaced metal ones on men's jackets, and have been reproduced in various sizes on women's tailor-mades and dresses. The latest suggestion, for the coming millennium, is that of a huge, smooth blue enamel button so perfect that it would seem velvety to the touch as well as to the eye.

171.172. Enamel invades almost all smart metal surfaces. Roberta di Camerino and Mila Schön call on Bomisa, of course, to enamel their belts.

173.174. Ken Scott, Moschino, Ferré, Gucci, Dior, Cartier and Yves Saint-Laurent sign their enamel buttons from the 70's onwards.

173.

174.

176.

175. Enamel buttons for sports clubs and elegant caprices.

176. The elegant enamel button also catches the eye of Gilles Dewavrin, a coming stylist who bases one collection on the theme of double buttoning. *Fashion*, supplement, 30 June 1987.

175.

17

177: A very delicate detail in making enamel buttons is that of finding the correct steel punch. Bomisa punches for enamel articles.

TOWARDS THE NEW MILLENNIUM

BUTTONS AND STYLE

The appetite for buttons shown by fashion-trends at the end of the Seventies spilled over into the next decade.

There was a great button revival in the men's clothing sector, which by the Seventies had become as conditioned by fashions as that of women, varying from one season to another. Once "oversized" jackets became the rage, the dimensions of buttons changed also, as did their colours, abandoning dark shades for brighter and more brilliant effects. Men's fashion groups and designers no longer left the choice of buttons for jackets, reefer-coats and overcoats to chance. Zegna, Giorgio Armani and Cerruti refused classic saucer-shaped buttons, and adopted forms more suitable to the new philosophy of clothes. By 1984 the look of buttons had changed, and they were now made of a synthetic resin often known as corozite, which imitated the natural corozo of recent memory.

178. The early 80's style brings back a sober-toned masculine elegance. Buttons revert to the classic four-holed variety. Gian Marco Venturi. Photo Aldo Fallai in *Uomo Vogue,* December 1985.

179.

180.

179.180. Buttons were rare in the general panorama until the mid-80's. Only Valentino used masses of them for his *Haute Couture* and *boutique* models and put metal or enamel ones on men's jackets and overcoats. *Harper's Bazaar* supplement to n. 3, March 1985.

181.

182.

181.182. A double row of very convex grey buttons to decorate the jacket (*Vogue Italia* advertisement) and another series, of old classic white Trocas, for Valentino boutique, blue and white outfit. *Harper's Bazaar,* cit.

183.

Soon after, with the first waves of the "new tide", the night-world came back into fashion, and evening dress came with it.

Dinner-jackets were modernized along lines of which the truly elegant did not always approve, and their buttons, which international good taste had always required to be entirely made of black braiding or silk, were now decorated with golden, jet or strass surrounds.

Women's styles continued to exaggerate the shoulders, widening the upper body enormously. There was a revival of leg-of-mutton sleeves. The early Eighties witnessed a Renaissance whim, with quantities of buttons on little jerkins over swelling skirts or puffed-out, pear- or melon-shaped trousers that seemed to come straight from a 16th century painting.

183.184. Button-styles for men in the early 80's are extremely discreet. Apart from metal and enamel buttons colour is only used on travelling clothes and sportswear.

ONE BUTTON LEADS TO ANOTHER

To the tune of "welcome back, Mister Button", the new collection made urgent calls for buttons, especially to Italian manufacturers who, for decades already, had held the place of honour for good taste and quality. Some observers attribute the explosion to Jean-Paul Gaultier, the French *enfant terrible*. English-speakers think it was Patrick Kelly, the Paris-based American designer, who launched the button-mania of the Eighties.

185.186. It is always said that Patrick Kelly started the latest "button-craze" and Balmain followed suit with stepped buttons. *Collezioni Alta Moda* n. 2 Spring-Summer 1987.

185.

186.

Whoever had the idea first, it was followed enthusiastically, and the story of fastenings was enriched by new approaches to function, even if purely decorative, and the materials, make, shape and colour of the new samples. The fifteen or twenty sorts of button that had adequately satisfied the needs of wholesalers and tailor's shops were quickly multiplied by hundreds: Luigi Fenili (of the second generation), when asked how many button types there were in his collection, shrugged his shoulders and said: "I don't know! There may be (20,000), but I lose count, because there are new ones every day".

The designers' decision to use non-metallic materials - resin, galalite, corozo, horn or mother-of-pearl - is nearly always taken in consultation with the manufacturer.

Why Karl Largerfeld or Franco Moschino prefer horn rather than resin or corozo is a mystery concerning the immediate interest of the button-maker. There's no need to enquire further, you'll never find out.

Technical drawings are submitted to the customer in the case of logos or personalized designs, and also if the maker would like to have his idea confirmed by the designer.

Angelo Fenili says that the Prealpino factory, which has belonged to his family for three generations, is one of the very few Italian establishments that still finishes its buttons by hand, and that the buttons are coloured exactly as they would be in a back-kitchen! The factory does, indeed, have a large kitchen in which powdered dyes are heated up in water. Other buttons are set out on trays, sprayed with colour and put in an oven to dry. Corozo buttons are very hygroscopic, and once dyed are put in the sun to dry, just like red peppers.

187. Scarlet roses for Ungaro's buttons. *Collezioni Alta Moda* n. 6 Spring-Summer 1988.

188. An overcoat by Emilio Cavallini in red wool bright as a Napoleonic Marshall's uniform. *Collezioni Uomo* n. 4 Autumn-Winter 1989-90.

189. Shiny buttons, too on Ferré's overcoat. *Collezioni Alta Moda* Autumn-Winter 1989-90.

116

187.

188.

189.

190.

191.

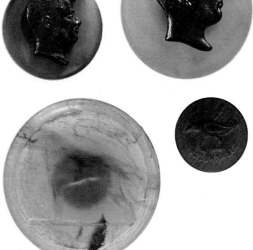

192.

ON WITH THE SHOW

The reappearance of buttons in an obviously decorative role has been heralded by the fashion-papers in a number of articles.

In 1987, the *Giornale d'Italia* published a piece by Anna Municchi, summing up the direction of the past three seasons in an imaginary fashion-parade.

"The revived and embellished button has triumphed on all de luxe sailor-styles (especially for town wear), and on blue tailor-mades, now the height of fashion. Mother-of-pearl buttons fasten Ferrè's waistcoats, worn one on top of the other without a shirt, and gilt buttons border the deep V-fronts of silk marocain.

Armani uses them to fasten his wide double-breasted short jacket with a baby-collar, worn with an organza skirt. Missoni has masses of buttons on the front of his summer *bustier*. Versace puts tiny strass

190.191. Martine Sitbon prefers mother-of-pearl, while Pierre Cardin, always evolving, likes eccentric buttons. *Collezioni Prêt-à-porter* n. 9 Spring-Summer 1989; *Collezioni Alta Moda* n. 6

192. A glamorous collection of sculpted horn buttons in three sizes, in which designer Franco Moschino appears a Roman Emperor. Bottonificio Prealpino.

193.

194.

ones on the front of his straight-up-and-down frocks as well as "sprinkling" them on jackets. Laura Biagiotti replaces her leather-belt buckle with a huge button, or "designs" them in jaquard on her *trompe l'oeil* pullovers. Luciano Soprani sews one or two rows of them on his sexy bathing-suits.

Gold is the password for Moschino (two buttons on the cuff-edge of his jeans and five on the flap of his American Marine trousers). Barocco and Gherardini put buttons on the back of a long Spring jacket to hold the panel. Krizia has big black-on-white buttons on her mini-redingote, and a single one to finish off the drape of her blue costume.

The youngest Italian designers all agree: Dolce and Gabbana have literally constellated a jersey suit with press-studs until it looks like "do it yourself" - you can shorten and drape it as you like. Practically speaking, you build it on your own body.

193.194. Buttons, buttons and more buttons for all button-crazy collectors. Lolita Lempicka, Paris. *Collezioni Prêt-à-porter* n. 9.

195. Buttons of synthetic material mixed with marble-dust to give a very effective geological look. Bottonificio Prealpino.

195.

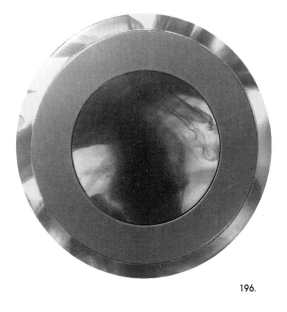

196.

197.

198.

199.

200.

201.

202.

But those who decided that "the more the merrier" were Luca Coelli and Sam Rey, with their *PourToi* collection. Half-measures have here been thrown to the winds. Some of their jumpers have up to 600 buttons, and, amazingly, are not too heavy as a result. They began quietly, "designing" with buttons (almost as an alternative to polka-dots in trimmings) in spirals, zig zag patterns or to complete an elegant jaquard outfit, but in their ethnic summer collection they used buttons as though they were bits of cork. "We were trying", they say, "to find something very primitive-looking". And this proved to be the triumph of mother-of-pearl buttons, used also as necklaces and often the wrong way round, showing the rough side. So buttons to the fore, buttons are beautiful! Among women fashion-writers, the smart evening-bag nowadays is completely covered in jewellery-buttons of the 50's. To sum up, buttons are not for mere fastening alone, but especially to look good, to ornament".

196.-202. At the end of the 80's buttons like these from the Bottonificio Prealpino are striking in their dimensions also. Models with large buttons by Mila Schön, Raniero Gattinoni and Jean-Paul Gaultier. *Collezioni Alta Moda* n. 6.

203.

PEARLY REFLECTIONS

It seems as though the pages of this long essay have been punctuated with the iridescent reflections of buttons, which first appeared in their precious form to fasten the coats and "camisiole" of 18th century gentlemen. The elegant use of mother-of-pearl buttons has never declined although the incomparable beauty of antique examples has lost some refinement through an almost indiscriminate and endless use.

At the end of the 20th century we are still arguing about mother-of-pearl and its qualities, even though, for reasons of cost, the *Meleagrina* has been replaced by the shells of the *Trocus*, called Trocas in the trade - more abundant in nature and easily found. The "fingernail" reflections of the rounded Trocas shell are very different from the precious "long rainbows" of the big flat *Meleagrina*.

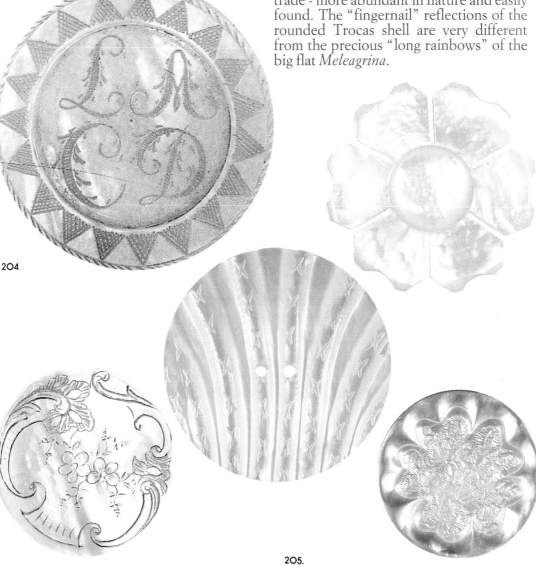

204.

205.

The most valuable mother-of-pearl comes from Australia: the subtle white variety with long, changing reflections, or the darker one, with an almost bronze hue. Another esteemed variety is that of Tahiti, which has grey-green gleams, sometimes described as "black".

However, nowadays only Trocas is worked, says Sergio Cannara, of the third generation of a firm active since 1931.

207.

203. Mother-of-pearl incised with steel decoration imitating brilliants. France mid-18th century.

204. Mother-of-pearl button is incised with a "naughty rebus": *Elle a cedé*. France 18th century.

205. Gold decoration follows the Art Nouveau style of the early 1900's; the other three buttons are of Australian mother-of-pearl from the 30's, 50's and 60's respectively; Italy.

206. Three buttons in Tahiti mother-of-pearl known as "black" from its grey-green iridescence. Italy, 60's and 80's.

207. Buttons of shell and casein (galalite). Italy, 30's.

208. Australian mother-of-pearl and Heliotis buttons. Italy, 30's and 50's.

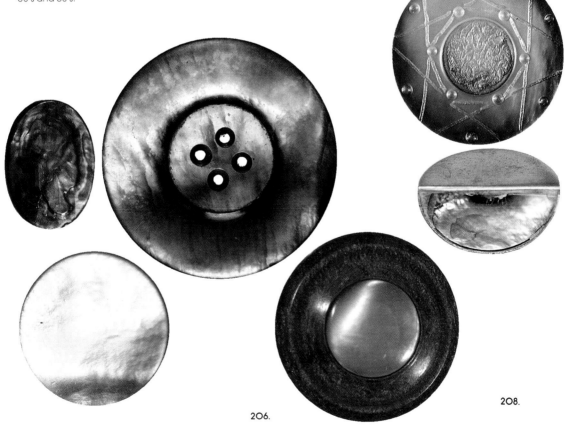

206.

208.

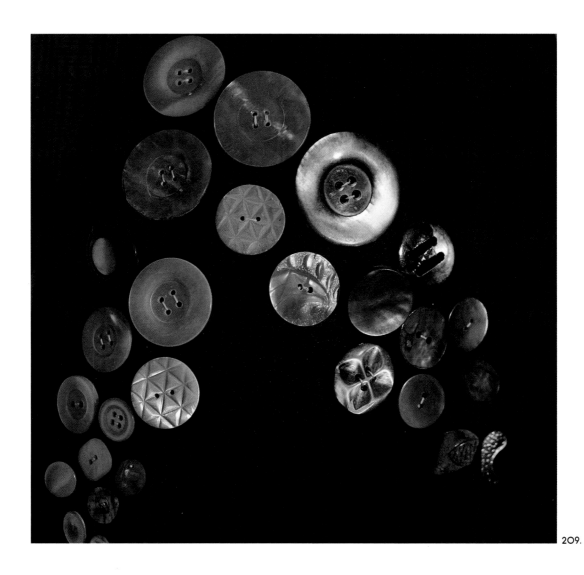

209.

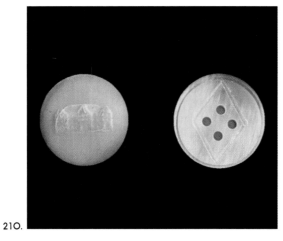

210.

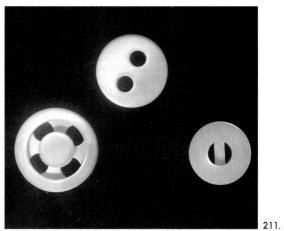

211.

209. Little mother-of-pearl and Trocas buttons for all domestic purposes.

210. 211. Little mother-of-pearl and Trocas buttons for shirts.

The long and delicate job begins with cutting discs from the shell. These are then graded, flattened by hand and turned on a semiautomatic lathe on each side. Once the little discs have been pierced, they already look like buttons, and are whitened in baths of hydrogen peroxide before being "roughed up" in cylinders with water and pumice-stone. A perfect shine is obtained with corozo-powder, after which the cycle is complete, and the vegetable matter used in the first industrial buttons has polished the most aristocratic buttons Mother Nature has given us.

All this is true for ordinary four - or two -holed buttons. Fashion and style have further requirements, to be satisfied by engraving the buttons with designs, and even, for a change, using the back instead of the polished surface. The Cannara factory also uses mother-of-pearl in wood or metal combinations to obtain brilliant, changing, sparkling effects.

Customers are all dress-designers, and on one occasion at least, thanks to Liviana Conti, smug buttons took on the festal iridescence of spangles: she sewed 800 Trocas buttons as sequins on a jersey, transforming a homely, sportswear jumper into an effervescent garment shining with a thousand rainbows.

There are still some people who want real mother-of-pearl ! Model 0I335, with four holes and 5mm thick, is made of Australian mother-of-pearl and adorns the shirts of Gianni Agnelli, and also those of Sergio Loropiana, who has no doubt about the great man's elegance and taste.

Silvio Berlusconi, however, keeps abreast of the time and always orders for his fine shirts the "Normal thin Trocas line 16", with pink back.

But that is not the whole story. Mr. Bijan is an oil-rich Iranian millionaire, who owns a chain of exclusive American men's shops for selected costumers (to whom he hands, so it is said, a golden key so that they can come in even when the shop is shut, and help themselves). He buttons his own shirts and those he sells with "white Australian" bordered with gold (real). This is a return to the button-as-jewel, rather like those kept lock and key by the house of Cartier, which made them in the Forties, and which are now greatly sought after by collectors, as well as those

produced more recently by Bulgari, the *via Condotti* jeweller, who showed in the early Eighties a collection of solid gold buttons, flat or convex, imitating braiding and sold in series of three large and two small ones, done up in satin and velvet boxes.

212. Three incised Trocas buttons. Italy, 30's.

212.

213.

213. At Bärnau in Germany mother-of-pearl buttons made from big *Meleagra* shells began to be produced in the 1890's.
Examples of buttons from the collection in Bärnau button-museum.

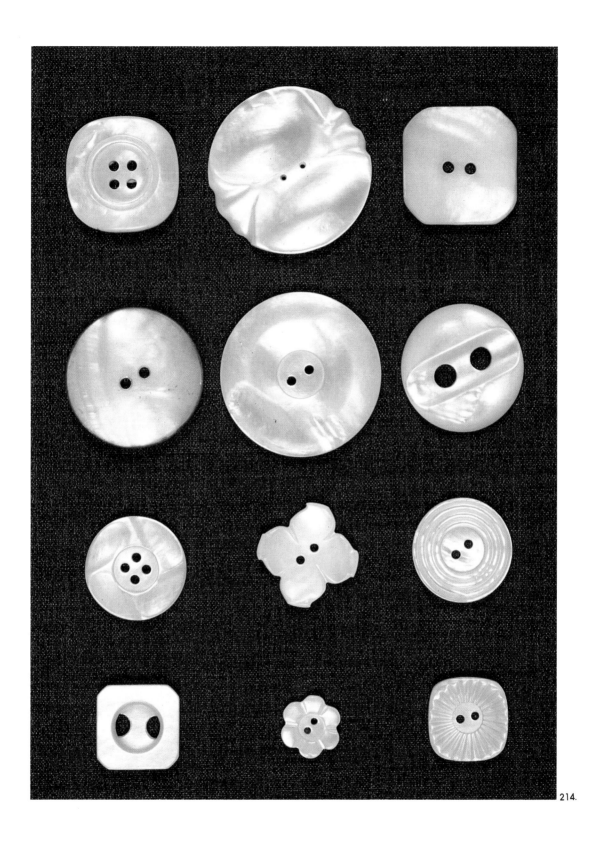

214. A panorama of mother-of-pearl lines for the 90's. Cannara. *Tessuto Collezioni* n. 1 Spring-Summer 1990.

214.

BUTTONS WHERE?

The 20th century draws to its close, elegant women are rediscovering the joy of buttons, changing them often on their dresses as they did in the '50's. The little disc, in all its metarmorphoses, has become a sought-after object, and not only when one has been lost.

Buttons are full of symbolic significance, and without going so far as the 18th century's conceits (L A C D to mean *Elle a cedé*, engraved on mother-of-pearl) they still contain messages. Buttons showing claws or the beaks of birds of prey have obviously been chosen by someone aggressive, or who at least wishes to become so. Filigree, spirals, crystal drops, mosaic decorations and the sheen of glass beads from Murano go with a timeless wish for beauty and fantasy.

The button-box children played with until the thirties, when it was laid aside in favour of more consumer- oriented toys, has returned to fashion, giving rise to new, fantastic, extraordinary collections.

The collecting-mania has caught on everywhere, and even the treasures that do not rival in size those of Baroness Rothschild (to be seen at Waddesdon Manor in England), are still worthy of our curiosity. There is a shop in France that is said to furnish the needs of a hundred collectors, and Romano Goni, who owns some fifteen thousand stupendous buttons of every kind, set out in hundreds of drawers, searches antique-shops and old haberdashers' (there are almost none left) to complete his already remarkable collection. As Goni himself cuts and polishes button-discs from plates and sticks of polyester and galalite, he has quite rightly begun to catalogue his own best pieces so as to provide a complete picture of the button-world.

128

215. "Dice" buttons on Patrick Kelly's suit were bought from *Tender Buttons* in New York. *Collezioni Alta Moda* n. 6.

215.

There are shops over the world over which can satisfy the strangest fixations of button-maniacs and also provide the right button to give the final note of elegance to an outfit. When Patrick Kelly walked into *Tender Buttons* in New York, and bought buttons made from dice, the owners of the shop, Millicent Safro and Diana Epstein, wondered when those buttons would appear on some of his dresses. They had not long to wait before he used the unusual shape to complete his clothes in the uninhibited American style of "chic".

In their tiny, treasure-filled shop, the two owners have been exploiting their mania for several decades. It is the only store of its kind in the city, and can meet the most extravagant requirements, even for a christening-button ordered by an Irish family. From the million of items, there came forth a tiny pearl with an even tinier shamrock on it, the whole thing measuring a quarter of an inch. Greta Garbo goes to *Tender Buttons* to buy buffalo-horn ones, Jane Powell those of strass and Calvin Klein buttons for his blazer - famous purchasers of buttons for all tastes, even those of the most sophisticated collectors, who wish to buy not button alone, but the story behind each one.

Since 1960, *Button Queen* in London has been selling collectors' buttons, those most in demand being *Art Nouveau* and *Art Déco*. To meet the needs of fashion-designers they have recently added "new" buttons, mainly from Italian factories, to their stocks.

The *Droguerie* in Paris buys and collects buttons from everywhere: from the Moon, if that were possible, after 1975. *Madame* Laguilhaumie helps homewives, collectors and dress designers from the world over, and the last-named buy the most extravagant ones to have them reproduced for their own models. Men of great elegance come to the shop to change the standard buttons on their shirts, and one of the most faithful customers is Inès de La Fressange, Chanel's star mannequin who continued for years to perpetuate the Chanel look. We imagine that she sought,

216. Inès de La Fressange "metallizes" according to the dictates of the Chanel style. *Collezioni Alta Moda* n. 10 Spring-Summer 1989.

216.

217.

219.

218.

220.

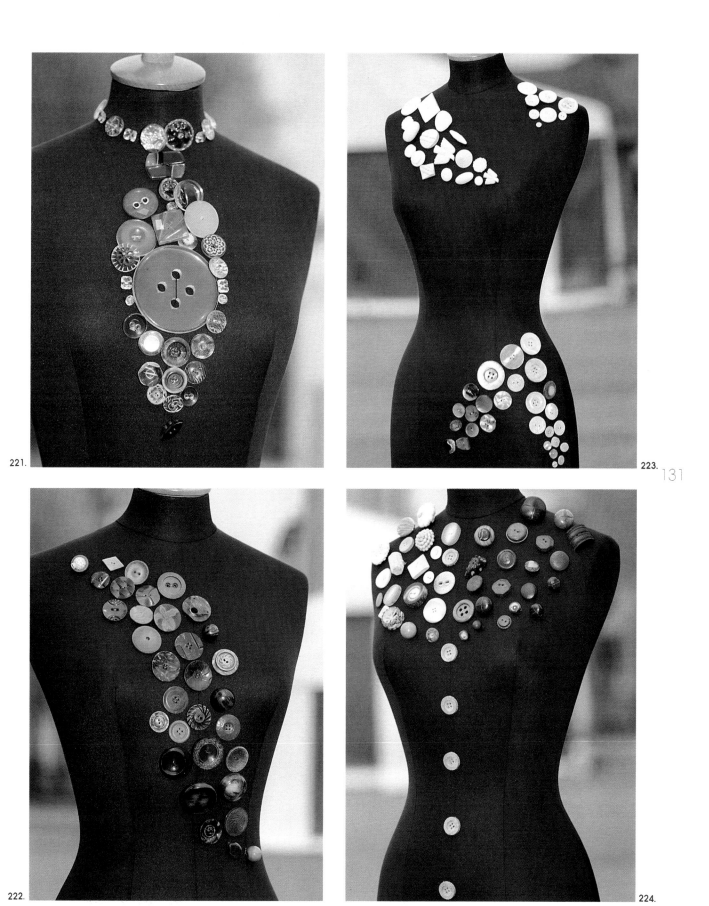

221.

223.

222.

224.

217.-224. Under the artistic direction of Michaela De Favari, Vittoria de Buzzaccarini presents her "harvest" of the 20th century buttons at the S.I.B.A. (Salone Internazionale del Bottone, Piacenza, Italy), 1989. Photo Giuliano Grossi

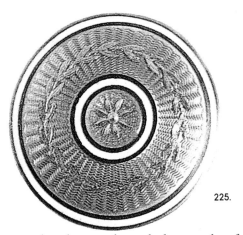

225.

226.

among the thousands and thousands of buttons there, these with the Assyrian lion's head made immortal by the immortal *Mademoiselle*.

Franco Jacassi in Milan also has marvellous examples of buttons, which would delight many collectors, but he keeps them under lock and key in orderly rows, as benefits so precious a collection, which is only put at the disposal of the aristocrats of *Haute Couture* and international fashion.

His preferences (and it is undeniable that buttons are like cherries, one leads to another and before you know it you have caught the mania yourself) are for material buttons of coloured silk interwoven with gold thread, and those made of opalescent coloured-glass paste and hand painted, which were produced in Czechoslovakia and Germany during the Twenties.

However, for Jacassi, the real button is made of resin or the industrial plastic of the Fifties - the Italian button *par exellence,* due to the dexterity and intelligence of Italian workers, which came to the fore in a winning combination with Italian fashion itself.

227.

225. *Basse-taille* enamel button by Cartier. 1920's. *Tender Buttons* collection.

226. A button incised in a cabochon crystal and mounted as a pin. Vittoria de Buzzaccarini Collection.

227. Lithographed button on metal. France, c. 1850, and two others hand-engraved and stamped of the 18th and 19th centuries, from the collection of R. Goni of the firm Miban.

228.

229.

BUTTONS FOR MUSEUMS

All museums of costume, even those without special collections of buttons, show them off on the clothes displayed. As these are always fine examples of their kind, the accessories naturally are fine also.

Special collections have been made of antique and historical buttons; revolutionary types at the *Musée Carnavalet* in Paris, Louis XV ones in the *Musée de l'Ile de France* in St.Jean-Cap Ferrat and at Caen, in the *Musée de la Normandie*.

In England, where Birmingham was the first centre of industral production, the *City Museum* has a button collection, and there is one in the Bath *Museum of Costume*. There are valuable French and English buttons in the *Musées Royaux d'Art et d'Histoire* in Brussels.

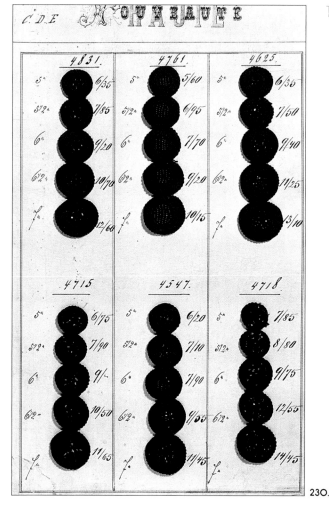

230.

228.229. Buttons with a mother-of-pearl base and enamelled metal decoration, peculiar to early 20th century taste, made by Bärnau factories and shown in the local button-museum.

230. Sample-cards of the late 18th century braided buttons from the *Museo del Costume*, Palazzo Mocenigo, Venice.

In Italy the Florence *Galleria del Costume* holds the "Donazione Tirelli", covering two centuries of costume-history down to the mid-18th century, with many interesting buttons on the clothes shown. There are buttons for every taste in the *Civiche Raccolte d'Arte* at Milan's Castello Sforzesco, and the Palazzo Mocenigo in Venice has many "cards" with samples of the black and coloured material-button fashionable at the end of the 19th century.

The collection at the *Metropolitan Museum of Art*, New York, may be seen by appointment. The owners of *Tender Buttons* (a shop) have donated a collection

232.

134

to the *Cooper-Hewitt Museum* there.

In Germany, private initiative led to the opening at Bärnau in the 70s of an historical museum completely devoted to this accessory. Since 1985, *Herr* Marcel Hermann, ex director of the professional button-makers school, has been holding in the school (now closed) special exhibitions dealing with specific sectors of button history. The 1985 show featured wood and corozo buttons; in 1986 came glass ones. Metal had its turn in the following year, which covered two thousand years of "fastenings". 1988's show of mother-of-pearl and its substitutes was followed in 1989 by all types of synthetics, from celluloid to the resins and polyesters provided for the industry by 20th century technology.

231. Revolutionary buttons of the end of the 18th century shown at the *Musée Carnavalet*, Paris.

232. Original 18th century buttons with copper framed polychrome feathers. *Municipal Collection*, Castello Sforzesco, Milano.

231.

BUTTON MADNESS

There were people who made an uniform of buttons, in the days when mother-of-pearl buttons were very fashionable in London and very cheap. In the 1880's, the head of a London charity having its roots in the Middle Ages and whose members were known as Pearlies, had the idea of decorating his trousers with a double row of mother-of-pearl buttons. This caught on, and soon other members of the association began sewing buttons on their clothes, including collars, lapels, trousers and entire waistcoats, of which the pocket-flaps provided an excellent field for this amusing button-fantasy. By the Nineties, mother-of-pearl-button madness was in full swing, involving wives also, who decorated their dresses with the buttons and their hats with the ostrich-feathers considered the height of elegance in the *Belle Epoque*. This went on until one day a member of the society covered a complete set of tails, bought second-hand for the purpose, with mother-of-pearl buttons, to which he added the appropriate top hat, patent shoes and cane. All this was very burdensome to wear, but the effect was electrifying, and henceforth the Pearly King and Queen appeared at all the fêtes of the association with their clothes wholly covered in buttons, from twenty to thirty thousand for a man's suit to as many as sixty thousand for a woman's evening dress.

233. A dress from the *PourToi* collection designed by Luca Coelli in 1987, decorated with Trocas buttons showing the "crust" side.

234. An original "costume" completely covered in buttons. *Deutsches Knopfmuseum,* Bärnau.

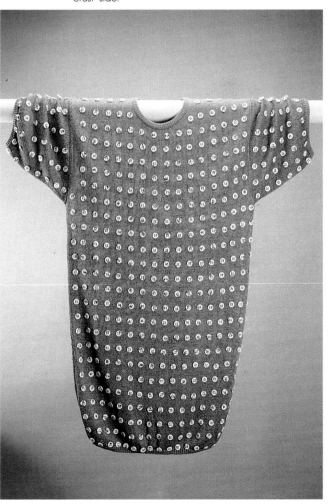

234.

A century later the Pearlies still have their charity, and still wear their buttons, except that, given the price of these today, they simply reproduce on the backs of men's jackets and the fronts of women's dresses symbolic designs that may vary from faith, hope and charity (the cross, anchor and heart), to lover's knots, shamrocks, sunbursts and rainbows. In order of precedence, it is the King who wears the pearly jacket, and the next in line, the Prince, has to be content with the waistcoat. All wear caps completely covered with mother-of-pearl buttons, and there have even been Pearly dogs with a little jacket, helping their master to collect for poor childrens' Christmas presents outside Victoria Station.

Buttons are beautiful and perhaps a bit mad too! says Annie Lennox, the blonde rock singer, who decorates the cuffs, shoulders and hems of her leather tails and trousers with mother-of-pearl and steel buttons, which combine to give off metallic flashes and iridescence.

Designer Piero Polato, however, favours a coloured-button *pot-pourri* to decorate a space-suit, in a send-up of the most sophisticated technology, - the Martian disguise to be completed by a puff of stardust for the face.

So it's true that, with buttons, "anything goes"!

But that's not the end of the story, nor of the possibilities that technology, fantasy and button-mania may think up for exploring ever new constellations in the Button Universe.

235. "Ironic Buttons", photo Circià-Perego. From the Swiss TV programme *Il Mascheraio*. P.Polato *Tutti in Maschera*.

236. The Pearly Queen celebrates the anniversary of her association properly adorned with mother-of-pearl buttons. *In Britain,* March 1973.

237.

237. Bomisa's proposal for the coming millennium is the macro-button, bright with enamel.

APPENDIX

GLOSSARY

ENGLISH

Acetates — *synthetic products used from the sixties onwards. Their low cost and ease of use allowed for mass production*

Argentan — *copper, zinc and nickel alloy*

Bakelite — *synthetic material discovered by Leo Hendrick Baekeland*

Polishing — *mechanical or manual polishing operation which does not remove chips of material*

Smoothing — *mechanical operation carried out in cylinders with water and pumice in order to smooth shell buttons*

Casein — *a coagulant found in milk. Its sublimation with fomaldehyde was discovered in 1903 and was used in button manufacturing from the end of the First World War. The term is often used as a substitute for "galalith" in the button context*

Celluloid — *first synthetic product invented in 1869 by John Hyatt of New Jersey*

Horn — *taken from buffalo, cattle and deer, in more special cases (buttons for Tyrolese or Austrian loden cloth): used for normal buttons or made into luxurious versions by engraving*

Vegetable ivory — *fruit of a tropical South American plant used for button-making*

Diamond wheel grinding — *a mechanical polishing operation carried out using tool with industrial diamonds*

Galvanic finishes — *plating with gold, nickel, copper, brass, silver etc. achieved by immersing products in electrolytic baths*

Flash — *galvanic finish in gold solution varying fom 580 to 680 x 1000*

Galalite — *casein - formaldehyde produced in sheets or bars for making into buttons*

Gross — *twelve dozen ie.144 pieces. Unit of measurement used for the sale of buttons*

Heliothis — *Shell with beautiful gleams. As highly prized as mother of pearl*

Engraving — *hand-crafting with a burin in order to reproduce the desired design on a die*

Line measure — *unit of measurement for button diameter: each line is equal to 0.65 mm*

Mother-of-pearl — *raw material taken from meleagrina shells*

Brass and tombac — *alloys of copper, lead, iron, aluminium, tin, silicon, manganese or nickel with various composition percentages*

Plexiglass — *transparent acrylic resin*

Polyester — *synthetic material prized for the ability to create different chromatic effects through the use of additives such as "pearl essence" which gives a translucent effect*

Polystyrene — *synthetic material used from the 1950's*

Ureic resin — *synthetic products which have taken the place of galalite since the forties*

Welding — *operation performed to join pieces of metal*

Trimming — *removal and rounding of surplus or sharp parts*

Enamel — *a button decoration method involving firing in a kiln. Enamelling has been used since the 18th century and usually creates designs on slightly concave metal surfaces*

"cloisonné — *this describes a design which is perfectly otulined with strips of metal. Colour is placed in each "cell"*

"basse-taille — *transparent glaze is applied to a metal surface which has been embossed, engraved or knurled*

Coining dies — *a block in various geometric shapes made from extremely hard steel, used for shaping buttons through coining*

Trimming dies — *a block in various geometric shapes made from extemely hard steel, used for defining the shape of buttons or the coined piece*

Tortoise-shell — *natural material used for buttons especially at the beginning of the 20th century*

Trocas — *commercial name of the Trocus shell which is used to make buttons that are like mother-of-pearl but of a lower quality*

Antirust glaze — *transparent glaze which protects metal from rusting.*

ITALIANO	FRANÇAIS	DEUTSCH	ESPAÑOL
Acetati	Acétates	Azetate	Acetatos
Alpacca	Argentan	Alpaka	Alpaca
Bakelite	Bakélite	Bakelit	Baquelita
Bornitura	Politur	Pulido	
Burlonatura	Polissage coquillages	Schleifen	Lijado
Caseina	Caséine	Kasein	Caseína
Celluloide	Celluloïd	Zelluloid	Celuloide
Corno	Corne	Horn	Cuerno
Corozo	Corozo	Elfenbeinnuß	Corojo
Diamantatura	Diamantage	Diamantieren	Diamantado
Finiture galvaniche	Finitions galvaniques	Oberflächengalvanisierung	Terminaciones galvánicas
Flash	Flash	Flash	Flash
Galalite	Galatithe	Galatith	Galalita
Grossa	Grosse	Gros	Gruesa
Heliotis	Héliothis	Heliothis	Heliotis
Incisione	Gravure	Einritzung	Incisión
Lineato	En ligne	Liniert	Lineado
Madreperla	Nacre	Perlmutter	Nácar
Ottone e Similoro	Laiton et similor	Messing und Scheingold	Latón y Similor
Plexiglass	Plexiglas	Plexiglas	Plexiglás
Poliestere	Polyester	Polyester	Poliéster
Polistirene	Polystyrène	Polystyrene	Poliestireno
Resine ureiche	Résine urée	Harnstoffharze	Resinas úricas
Saldatura	Soudure	Schweißen	Soldadura
Sbavatura	Ebarbage	Entgräten	Desbarbado
Smalto	Email	Glasur	Esmalte
"cloisonné	Cloisonné	Cloisonné	"cloisonné"
"basse-taille	Basse-taille	Basse-Taille	"basse-taille"
Stampi di conio	Moule de frappe	Prägestempel	Troquel
"di rifilo	De coin	Schabeschnitt	Molde
Tartaruga	Tortue	Schildkröt	Carey
Trocas	Trocas	Trocas	Trocas
Zaponatura	Vernissage	Zaponlackierung	Barnizado

BIBLIOGRAPHY

BOOKS

1581 - F. Caroso, *Il Ballerino*, Venezia

1832 - G. Ferrario, *Il Costume* di *tutti i popoli antichi e moderni*, Firenze

1860 - *Raccolta Ufficiale delle Leggi e dei Decreti del Regno d'Italia*

1863 - *Vocabolario degli Accademici della Crusca*, quinta impressione, Tipografia Galileiana, Firenze

1913 - F. Malaguzzi Valeri, *La corte di Ludovico il Moro*. Ed. Hoepli, Milano

1923 - *Manuale del fabbricante di bottoni e di pettini, articoli in celluloide e in galalite,* edito sotto l'alto patronato del Ministero dell'Insegnamento Tecnico

1923 - *Raccolta Ufficiale delle Leggi e dei Decreti del Regno d'Italia*, Libreria dello Stato, Roma

1928 - M. von Böhn, *La Moda*, Salvat editores, Barcelona

1928 - *Raccolta Ufficiale delle Leggi e dei Decreti del Regno d'Italia*, Libreria dello Stato, Roma

1931 - *Raccolta Ufficiale delle Leggi e dei Decreti del Regno d'Italia*, Libreria dello Stato, Roma

1935 - A.Parent, *Le bouton à travers les ages,* Ed. Alépée et C.ie, Paris

1949 - L.Smith Albert-K.Kent, *The Complete Button Book,* Doubleday & C., New York

1953 - F.Federici a cura di, *Enciclopedia della Famiglia*, Arnoldo Mondadori, Milano

1964 - R. Levi Pisetzsky, *Storia del Costume in Italia*, Treccani, Milano

1967 - S. C.Luscomb, *The Collector's Encyclopedia of Buttons*, Crown Publishers Inc., New York

1971 - *Il bottone italiano nel mondo*, Atti dei lavori del convegno: Il bottone italiano nel mondo, Piacenza, 24 aprile

1974 - L.Carluccio, *Domenico Gnoli*, Fabbri Editori, Milano

1974-75 - *I creatori della Moda e l'industria del bottone* Anno IX-n.2 ott. Anno X- n.1 apr. 1975; Anno X-n.2 ott. 1, Ed. Ariminum Grafica Editoriale, Milano

1976 - AA.VV., *Società e costume*, collana di X voll., Utet, Torino

1977 - AA.VV. *Rassegna di studi e notizie*, Raccolta delle stampe A.Bertarelli. Raccolte di Arte Applicata. Castello Sforzesco, Milano

1977 - V. Houart, *Buttons, A Collector's Guide*, Souvenir Press, London

1978 - R.Levi Pisetzky, *Il costume e la moda nella società italiana*, Einaudi, Torino

1978 - P.Peacock, *Discovering Old Buttons*, Shire Pubblications LTD, London

1979 - G.Bianchini, *Modelli di internazionalizzazione della produzione*, Franco Angeli, Milano

1981 - G.Butazzi, *Moda Arte Storia Società*, Gruppo Editoriale Fabbri, Milano

1981 - E. Charles-Roux, *Chanel and her World*, Weidenfeld and Nicolson, London

1981 - *Le Uniformi Italiane secondo il codice Cenni*, Editoriale Nuova, Novara

1982 - N.Aspesi, *Il Lusso & l'Autarchia*, Rizzoli, Milano

1983 - *La Galleria del Costume* (catalogo della collezione di Palazzo Pitti), Centro Di, Firenze

1983 - W.Packer, *I Grandi Disegnatori di Vogue* 1922-1982, Idealibri, Milano

1983 - U.Pericoli, *Le Divise del Duce*, Rizzoli, Milano

1984 - T.Gandouet, *Boutons*, Editions de l'Amateur, Paris

1985 - V.de Buzzaccarini, *La Sartigianeria*, Modart, Monza

1985 - P.Polato, *Tutti in Maschera*, Arnoldo Mondadori, Segrate Milano

1985 - *Tessuti, costumi, e moda*. Le raccolte storiche di Palazzo Mocenigo, Stamperia di Venezia

1985 - W. Wilson, *Man at His Best*, Esquire Press, New York

1985-86 - D. Testa, *L'industria bottoniera in Italia*, tesi di laurea, Università degli Studi di Parma

1986 - P. White, *Elsa Schiaparelli: Empress of Paris Fashion*, Aurum Press, London

1987 - *I Lanfranchi a Palazzolo*, Franco Maria Ricci, Parma

1987 - A. Municchi, *Eleganti e Abbottonatissime*, da *Il Giornale d'Italia* 25 febbraio p.19

1987 - F. Faggioni, *Chi ti attacca il bottone*, da Europeo, 3 ottobre

1987 - *Il libro del Sarto della Fondazione Querini Stampalia Venezia*, Panini, Modena

1988 - R. Martin, *Fashion and Surrealism*, Thames & Hudson, London

1988 - M. Tosa, *Vestiti da Sera... 1940*, Zanfi Editori, Modena

1989 - V. de Buzzaccarini, *Pantaloni & Co.*, Zanfi Editori, Modena

1989 - N. Pellegrin, *Les Vêtements de la Liberté*, Alinea, Aix-en-Provence

1989 - N. McCarty, *Tender Buttons* da *Almanac*, Franklin Mint, New York

s.d. - P.L. Giaferri, *L'Histoire du Costume Féminin Français*, Editions Nilsson, Paris

CATALOGUES

1979 - *The Liberty Stile*, Academy Editions, London

1986 - *Anziehungskräfte*, Münchner Stadmuseum, München

1986 - *Donazione Tirelli*, Arnoldo Mondadori, Milano

1986 - *Mestieri e Arti a Venezia*, 1173-1806, catalogo della mostra documentaria organizzata dall'archivio di Stato di Venezia, Tipografia Helvetia, Venezia

1987 - *L'abito della Rivoluzione*, Marsilio, Venezia

1988 - *Walter Albini, lo stile nella moda*, Zanfi Editori, Modena

MAGAZINES

1875 - 1878 : *Bazar, il Giornale delle Famiglie*

1889 - 1899 : *La Mode Illustrée*

1898 - 1900 : *La Saison*

1905 : *Les Modes*

1900 - 1917 : *La Mode Illustrée*

1908 - 1914 : *Fémina*

1910 : *Modes Parisiennes*

1912 - 1914 : *Le Journal des Dames et des Modes*

1918 - 1939 : *Vogue*

1920 - 1939 : *Fémina*

1929 - 1948 : *Le Jardin des Modes*

1938 - 1939 : *Gemma*

1939 - 1975 : *Grazia*

1940 : *Harper's Bazaar*, october

1942 - 1957 : *Bellezza*

1943 : *Fili Moda*, giugno

1949 : *L'Officiel*, avril

1949 - 1950 : *Marie Claire*

1946 - 1985 : *Annabella*

1951 - 1958 : *La Moda Maschile*

1952 : *Harper's Bazaar*, february

1973 : *In Britain*, march

1987 - 1990 : *Collezioni Alta Moda*

1987 - 1990 : *Collezioni Prêt-à-porter*

1988 - 1990 : *Collezioni Uomo*

1987 : *Europeo* 3 ottobre

1987 : *Il Giornale d'Italia*, mercoledì 25 febbraio

1989 : *Almanac*, september-october

1989 : *Tessuto Collezioni*

Printed in april 1990 by Malagoli Grafiche s.r.l. - Modena
Paper: CTS - Cartiera del Timavo e del Sole S.p.A. - Assago (MI)